WHO IS IN THE HOUSE?

WHO IS IN THE HOUSE?

A Psychological Study of Two Centuries
of Women's Fiction in America,
1795 to the Present

SALLY ALLEN McNALL

Department of English
The University of Kansas
Lawrence, Kansas

ELSEVIER
New York • Oxford

Exclusive Distribution
throughout the World by
Greenwood Press, Westport,
Ct. U.S.A.

Elsevier North Holland, Inc.
52 Vanderbilt Avenue, New York, New York 10017

Sole distributors outside the U.S.A. and Canada:
Elsevier Science Publishers, B.V.
P.O. Box 211, 1000 AE Amsterdam, The Netherlands

© 1981 by Elsevier North Holland, Inc.
Library of Congress Cataloging in Publication Data

McNall, Sally Allen.

Who is in the house? A psychological study of two centuries of women's fiction in
    America, 1795 to the present.
    "An Elsevier professional publication."

    Bibliography: p.
    Includes index.
    1. Women in literature. 2. American fiction—Women authors—History and
    criticism. 3. Popular literature—United States—History and criticism.
    4. Women—Psychology. 5. Women—United States—History. I. Title.
PS374.W6M3   813'.009'9287   80-26601
ISBN 0-444-99081-X

Copy Editor   Cynthia Carter
Desk Editor   Louise Calabro Schreiber
Design   Edmée Froment
Design Editor   Glen Burris
Mechanicals/Opening pages   José Garcia
Production Manager   Joanne Jay
Compositor   U.S. Lithograph
Printer   Haddon Craftsmen

Manufactured in the United States of America

To Mary Jeanette and Margaret Lucy,
to Mary, Pam, and Camilla,
to Betsy and Laurie,
to Marilyn, Michelle, and Melissa,
to Amy.

CONTENTS

PREFACE

What is a woman? A child, male or female? A family? What are sexual relations? What is marriage? Work? Love? The home? These questions are answered fully in the popular fiction written by and for women of the United States during the last two centuries. American women of the middle class, those with just enough leisure to read or to write, or possessing the resources that have allowed them to write for money, show us what it was and is like to be a mother or a daughter in the modern family during, and after, the period of industrialization.

This type of fiction speaks, of course, to and for the mass of women. It tells what they want to keep just as it is, what they can barely endure but cannot imagine changing, and what they would like to see changed. Popular fiction often seems to help its writers and readers accept social and psychological change. It does not crystallize popular ideology; it works at making it livable. It is a part of the history of the American family, and it is data that feminist theorists of the family cannot do without, but this book is not such a history, nor is it a theory of modern motherhood. It is, rather, an examination of how most women have thought and felt about themselves in our society.

The psychological part of the research for this study was funded by a fellowship from the Institute for Human Values in Medicine, which permitted me access to classes and books at the Topeka

Institute for Psychoanalysis and at the Menninger School of Psychiatry, as a fellow in the Menninger Foundation's Interdisciplinary Studies Program. Among the staff, I found particular inspiration in the work and conversation of Donald Rinsley and Carlos Estrada. The women, staff and patients, who became my friends and inspiration while I worked there, know who *they* are. John McCarthy deserves gratitude for his assistance during my two harried periods of research at the Library of Congress. I also wish to thank Scott McNall, Joe Hawes, Betsy Kuznesof, Marilyn Brady, and Dick McKinzie for reading early drafts.

WHO IS IN THE HOUSE?

1

THE INNER WORLD

I. The Historical Context

Popular women's fiction is a storehouse of material about modern woman's subjective sense of self. Until quite recently, however, even feminist literary scholars and historians have shied away from these books, preferring to concentrate on the feminist works that emerged concurrently with them.[1] Popular fiction, it is assumed, merely gives pleasure to the reader: not even the difficult pleasure of a unique vision, nor of new esthetic appreciations. Yet it does offer more than such a simple sort of pleasure, as we will see. Its enjoyment belongs not to the changing outer world, which "serious" fiction struggles to keep pace with, understand, and transcend, but to the relatively static inner world of wish and fantasy. Moreover, a popular novel is written to sell, and sell widely. It is a consumption article. Popular British and American novels written by and for women first appeared during the years when England and America were in the process of becoming industrial nations.[2] They, and the books like them which followed, form an invaluable record of the era during which our society, and family structure in our society, began to become "modern."

The usual view of the period before the American Revolution is that women of all classes were central to the country's economy, for it was still basically an agricultural home economy.

Woman was mistress of the household. Her husband was dependent on her labor in the household, and she also made money by exercising a variety of nondomestic skills—for example, textile manufacture, brewery, hostelry, trade, and medicine. The family was conceived of as an integral economic unit; all its members who could, worked in support of each other. The relationship between husband and wife was (at least in theory) one of equality; they chose each other and were companions.[3] Not the least of a wife's duties was, of course, to bear and raise children. At least in the Northern colonies, however, the father's duties in raising them (particularly sons, after the age of seven or so) were considered of nearly equal importance.[4] Such a schema de-emphasizes the role of patriarchal domination. In sharp contrast, during the rise of the modern nuclear family in the 19th century, men worked in the "public" sphere to support the "private" sphere of the home. Women and children therefore became economic dependents on their husbands and fathers.

Despite its simplicity, this sharp distinction defines the social world of popular women's fiction. Until about 1820, American fiction of this sort was indistinguishable from that produced in already industrialized England, and popular British novels sold well on this side of the Atlantic. One view of the developing British market for these books describes how the "confinement of women in the interior world of the family left bourgeois man 'free' to accumulate capital," leaving bourgeois woman "free to stay home and read."[5] These developments took place later in America,[6] and American middle-class women did not become a leisure class to the same degree as did their British counterparts.[7] Nevertheless, in the early national period and after, development toward an "interior world of the family" fostered the sort of common denominators of the inner world of the imagination that made—and make—popular fiction possible.

Since the middle of the 18th century, then, "women's books" have been aimed at certain responses in readers, certain desires and dreams that are shared by the majority of women. Books written in each popular genre I will describe are regularly, redundantly, rigorously, alike; the themes and images that I analyze are repeated from genre to genre. I have chosen groups of texts from the last two centuries of publication in America. Some texts I use, like Rowson's *Charlotte Temple*, Warner's *The Wide, Wide World*, Prouty's *Stella Dallas*, and Stratton-Porter's *A Girl of the Limberlost*, were so very popular in their day that they still enjoy a certain notoriety. Others have sunk from best-sellerdom into obscurity; still others never rose from obscurity although they enjoyed a limited vogue while their genre flourished.

Human beings in any society begin their lives in the care of their mothers or other females. Yet in America, in the period of time covered by this study, motherhood has been significantly transformed. Popular fiction, as I have said, does not really deal with changes in the outer world of historical development; in fact, it typically makes superficial adjustments to change, while retaining the basic structural formula.[8] These books are evidence and illustration of widespread and powerful cultural stereotypes, and of gradual transformations in these stereotypes over time.

As yet there is little agreement among historians of the family concerning the causes of transformations in family life.[9] I deal here with fictional stereotypes of the relationships of the generations and of the sexes, as they deeply resist change and as they reflect it. The involvement of these stereotypes with unconscious fantasy material is great, and therefore they are descriptive of the ways in which real American families, historically, have retained a certain form, not always by the conscious choice of the individuals who have been part of them.

II. The Content of the Fiction

The concept of women's economic dependency in our society is established in a collective ideology that operates at an unconscious level and draws much of its strength from the female child's special experience of dependency on her mother. In each social and historical context I work with, one common theme recurs: the young woman's ambivalence about growing up to be a woman. The fiction I will describe symbolizes this ambivalence in different ways, but always quite clearly.[10] The earliest human anxieties and mechanisms of defense are regular elements of construction in the emotional experience of popular women's fiction. The same may of course be said of any popular genre, but it is *women's* fiction that returns obsessively to the theme of willing/unwilling dependency, investing it with horror and anguish, ecstasy and bliss, interweaving it with dramas of pursuit, punishment, imprisonment, and escape. Has there been something special about American women's developmental histories in the centuries in question making it hard for them to become adult? The fiction appears to give positive evidence.

In the gothic and sentimental novels that are precursors to the ones I will discuss; in the "new gothic" in paperback; and in each popular form of women's fiction in the years between, plots reiterate, while characters and settings illustrate, the idea that it is at once absolutely necessary and extraordinarily difficult to keep a young woman in the home. The internal dynamic (and, I suggest, the economic history) of dependency and freedom determine the structure of these books.

There seems reason to believe that society is presently evolving a new dynamic of dependency and freedom, as a consequence of changes in economic realities. Psychic structure, in other words, may be reforming itself in accord with changes in the social structure, as it did at the beginning of the capitalist era,[11] under industrialization. Have traditions in popular women's fiction changed notably since their beginnings? The characters and elements of the "new gothic" do bear significant resemblances to their earlier fictional forms. On the other hand, a substantial number of popular novels from earlier decades of this century bear no traces of the "gothic" genre. Why is this so? Has it anything to do with the ideology of motherhood? This question will take the whole book to answer.

The ideology of motherhood under industrial capitalism may be seen in its most exacerbated form in the bourgeois nuclear family in the middle of the 19th century, the model of the social world that our authors all use. The limitations imposed by this model upon the self-concept of young women (not to speak of older ones) are many. The clinical literature documents them in frightening detail, and feminist analysis does no less. When psychoanalysis is used as a critical tool by the social scientist or historian, the *oedipal moment* (the acceptance, by boy or girl child, of the incest taboo and his or her sexual category, closing off other possibilities) is seen as the moment when a good bourgeois member of the social order is "produced."[12] And just here the girl's situation is the more difficult. She learns that what she has experienced as the incest taboo on her first love object is confirmed by the heterosexual society's taboo on all women. This is harder than the boy's discovery that all men are taboo, because she must now learn to love her mother in a different way if she is to have a secure identity. Moreover, she must obtain the help of her father if she is to learn to accept and deal with the masculine dominance of the patriarchal society.[13] To follow a female child through these difficulties, we need to go back to the years before the oedipal moment, to the time when her one love object is simply her mother, and the love object is the same for both infants.

The system in which mothers alone have the responsibility for child care reached its maximum rigidity in the families of the middle class in Western industrial society, particularly in the United States. This "peaking" of emphasis on the social role termed *motherhood* is the social and economic context of this book—what led up to it, and what succeeded it. We will see that as a mother's responsibility toward her children (especially her daughters) increased, so did the literary use of symbolic ways of warding off the fears and guilts and rages engendered by that situation.[14] Even in the late 1970s, women's popular fiction still depends on symbols of imprisonment, betrayal, escape—and on the old stereotypes of masculine rapacity and feminine passivity: the human child's greed and weakness translated into the terms of romantic love. By the time we have looked at selected precursors of the "new gothic," we will have some understanding of the reasons for this cultural lag. Both early childhood experience and the economic realities of the present will be seen as working to maintain women's "old-fashioned" sense of self.

The historical/literary facts about sentimental and gothic fiction, and the

19th century American domestic novel, are on record.[15] I am not concerned with describing these as such. This book is an interpretation of content, rather than a poetics of form; it is, therefore, a psychology of literature, making use of two models of psychological development just so far as they are descriptive of what I take to be the psychological content or themes of the fiction. As Rubin and Pratt have pointed out, and Mitchell demonstrated, any sufficiently descriptive theory can be used critically against itself, when that is necessary.[16] Ultimately, in this study, it *will* be necessary, but for the time being we can make some uncritical use of psychological theory's descriptive powers.

III. Developmental Models and the Analysis of Fiction

Freudian critics have been fond of analyzing the artist behind the work, and the evidences of conflict that remain in the work. More recently, they have turned their attention to similar data on the reader.[17] In either case, criticism is used to illustrate a model of human development that is, like the traditional "serious" realistic novel, a way of consciously connecting event to event and seeing a dynamic process there.

For popular fiction a somewhat different approach is needed. The Jungian critic's characteristic concentration on imagery and symbol shifts our attention from the plot to what the plot is about, from history to stereotype. Jung held "a concept of stadial development, each stage of which is determined by a particular instinctual 'archetypal' constellation."[18] Such constellations will be plentifully illustrated in the pages that follow. Jung said that "in the measure that the author is unconscious" of his or her "deeper meaning," narrative challenges the psychologist.[19] The authors of the narratives discussed in this study have been unconscious of some of their deeper meanings, especially those concerned with the experience of dependency on the mother. It is my task to sort out some of their unconscious capitulations and resistances to things as they were, and are, for women in the United States. Ideology, which Jungians call "collective consciousness," nevertheless often operates at an *un*conscious level, most notably when it matches unconscious formations as neatly as our *ideas* about motherhood match our early *fantasies* about it. Thus cultural stereotypes or imperatives, and archetypes in the Jungian sense, strengthen one another.

The body of psychoanalytic theory that most stimulates me in this endeavor is not Jungian, however. It is the work of the object–relations school, specifically the ideas of Klein, and of some recent American contributors.[20] These writers and thinkers focus on internalized interpersonal relationships—that is to say, early experiences within the bourgeois nuclear family—in contrast to the Freudian concept of drives. Their reasons for emphasizing the first two years of life can be gathered from an outline of

Margaret Mahler's description of what she has termed the *separation–individ-uation process*. Before the process itself occurs, there is a stage of *normal symbiosis* between mother and child, lasting until the infant is four or five months of age. During this stage, the infant has not yet developed ego boundaries, and experiences the mother as part of a world in which the differentiation between "I" and "you" has not yet been established. Psycho-logically speaking, this is the "primal soil from which all subsequent human relationships form." The separation–individuation phase that follows "is characterized by a steady increase in awareness of the separateness of the self and the 'other' which coincides with the origins of a sense of self, of true object relations, and of awareness of a reality in the outside world."[21]

In the view of these theorists, during our years of early dependency, our fantasies (and hence the deepest layer of our memories and fantasies as adults) are of a wildly dramatic nature, all black and white, and violently emotional—rather like popular fiction. Our first mental representations of the mother are of a "good object" and a "bad object," the being who is there taking proper care of our needs, and the one who is absent or rejecting or stifling. To these (eventually repressed) images are attached two conflicting mental representations of self (also eventually repressed)—one loving, good, and compliant, and one hating, bad, and guilty.[22] The main developmental task is to integrate the two sets of images.

The Jungian model is also one of integration, which says a great deal about *dis*-integration. What are the stages of the developmental process that Jung called individuation? What constellations of imagery signal their arrival and passing, and can be expected to signal pivotal points in a literary narrative about a human life? To begin with, a striking difference from psychoanalyti-cally conceived developmental phases is that Jung's process of individuation deals with adult experience, rather than that of the infant and child.[23] The process begins when the adult becomes aware that he or she has a *persona*, or a socialized role to which he or she is habituated. Breaking down these facades is the first stage in the process of individuation.

The second stage is the confrontation with the *shadow*, the "unrecognized dark half of the personality."[25] On the way to individuation, one must learn to recognize and accept it, in both its positive and negative aspects. The next stage, for a woman, is the discovery of the *animus*, or within a man, of the *anima*. These contrasexual figures also appear in positive and negative aspects and, like the shadow, are fantasized and/or projected upon others, sometimes playing out their roles in the rigid symbolic dramas of family pathology.

Clearly, thus far, there are provocative overlaps between Jungian and object–relations theory: Jung's idea of the shadow's positive and negative aspect, and those of the anima and animus, are similar to the ideas of good and bad representations of self and other. Jung, like Melanie Klein, assumes that the child and adult view the world as good/bad from some inherent disposition, an "irreducible fact" of the human mental constitution.[26]

According to the psychoanalytic model of the development of mental structure, we acquire our "internal objects," or mental representations of self and other, by three different processes. The earliest is the fantasy of actual oral incorporation. Slightly later, along with the defense mechanism of projection, introjection occurs. Objects are taken into the inner world that are progressively more whole, and more "realistic" assessments of the other. Finally, these mental representations—to simplify drastically—are identified with a more or less whole and stable sense of self; whereas the internalizations based on the earlier fantasies exist in a more or less permanent state of conflict with each other and of course with the sense of self.[27]

The points I wish to emphasize here are, first, the fantastic nature of the internalized object at each development stage, and, second, their persistence in adult mental life. I speak of dreams or fears of total satisfaction and security, mortal peril, fusion with an all-powerful goodness, and complete annihilation. The hunger and consequent "aggression" that we experience at the early stage of incorporation are overwhelming, terrifyingly so, and leave behind them terror about the damage we can do, or have done.[28] This early fear about ourselves is no more accessible to rational interpretation than our persistent longing for the perfect love of early fantasy. These are our psychic realities. With growth toward adulthood they may be layered over with thoughts of being dangerous, even poisonous; of being trapped; of being left, empty, or of service. But they are still there, and can be tapped by stories with related themes, to make us respond to these stories with powerful emotions.[29]

There is a risk involved in making connections between such assumptions about our mental processes and the facts of literary convention, formula, or genre. A book is, of course, an interaction between writer, text, reader, and the contexts of all three. To claim, as I do, that character, setting, and plot in popular women's fiction in America illustrate again and again some element in the early crisis of separation–individuation, is to concentrate on one among many interrelationships. My reason for choosing this emphasis is my belief that that early crisis, and its recapitulations in the youth and adulthood of the women who wrote and read these books, has been especially acute. I think we need to try to understand why that has been so, and a part of that understanding is what this book is intended to achieve.

IV. The Fictional Form

It will come as no surprise that the contents of the stories that lend the most credibility to a psychological theory allow them to be grouped under the formal heading of *romance*. According to one critic, "the romance form always shadows forth a regressive journey inward and backward . . . threatening the dissolution of the adult ego, while the novel form resists and punishes such dissolution."[30] A number of other definitions of the romance form fit our stories,[31] but this one takes us most directly into our subject. "The regressive disintegration of the self in romances," Bratlinger continues, "comes from internal forces . . . a paradoxical triumph over external circumstances in the midst of chaos, madness, and death."[32] The emphasis on the element of character, of the self, is important, since in these books we will find similar types, illustrating a similar dis-integration of self into a cast of "flat" characters rather than the novel form's "rounded" or whole, complex, characters. Bratlinger's idea of "paradoxical triumph" holds interesting implications for the variety of plot types in these texts, while "chaos, madness and death" recur regularly enough to be termed components of their physical settings, most often in a sense of external reality as chaotic, meaningless, and fatally dangerous.

In the romance form characters are not, then, the "living," autonomous-seeming wholes whom we feel we recognize or are even puzzled by on the pages of successful realistic novels. In a romance, plot is more important,[33] since it shows how the dream or desire of the hero or heroine is frustrated or satisfied. The hero or heroine embodies that desire; his or her other "characteristics" are incidental, even absent. Relationships with other characters or with the setting are determined by efforts to realize dream or desire, and not much by other contingencies. If this central character has problems with health, money, work, travel, and lodging, these are blatantly images and analogs of the central conflict.

The heroines of the popular romance forms discussed here are stereotypes then—more or less empty outlines into which intense emotion may flow. As Iser points out, "with a literary text we can only picture things which are not there; the written part of the text gives us the knowledge, but it is the unwritten part that gives us the opportunity to picture things."[34] It is Iser's impression that a predictable text, or one organized in rigid patterns, may be classified as subliterary because it does not provide for the "absorption of the unfamiliar" which is the true end of literature.[35]

All depends on what is meant by "the unfamiliar." In popular women's fiction, the "unfamiliar" is not a new approach to literary meaning, or even an experience new to the reader, but a scarcely surfacing "picturing of the unwritten"—indeed, of the unspoken, perhaps of the unthought because it is unthinkable. Here, the very predictability of these stories and their heroines means that the emotion of our most deeply buried fantasy life can emerge safely; we know it will be put away properly at story's end.

The human image is, then, in these stories, split into its component parts. Some are the familiar respectable ideals we cherish for ourselves and others (what Jung called personae) with which it is easy for the reader to identify in the ordinary sense of the word. Others are plainly not only unfamiliar but downright uncanny[36]—the rejected, disowned, and denied images of self and other—the "shadow"; the "bad part-object"; the horrifying inadmissible image of the "not-me"; and the unused potential and unacknowledged superiority in oneself, and others as well.[37] The appeal of popular women's fiction lies largely in the unparalleled opportunity it presents not only for a release of the usually repressed, but for a temporary healing of the splits in the personality, a provisional integration of parts. Their conventional plots, looked at from this perspective, represent more than just a willing affirmation of society's demands.

However, they have never represented a rebellion against such demands. None of these plots, because they *are* romance plots, can move their "part-characters" to a real completion in any model of psychological development.[38] Let us first look again at the Jungian model, the process of individuation. If one succeeds at the first three tasks, recognizing and distinguishing self from persona, recognizing and accepting the shadow self, and recognizing and integrating the contrasexual element, only one task remains. That is individuation itself, or, as it is sometimes called, the transcendent function, the experience of a Self which exists beyond the sum of human parts. In object–relations theory, the essential preliminary to integration of split images is a complete and completed process of mourning for our earliest love, the mother of our child-minds and emotions,[39] whom we must relinquish as we attempt to acquire adult minds and emotions.

In the chapters that follow, it will become clear that no plot formula of popular women's fiction allows for the completion of either of these developmental tasks, but rather formalizes an image of a heroine who does not recognize shadow nor contrasexual self, and who engages herself in the life-long task of propitiating an unmourned-for, unintegrated image of her mother. It is a commonplace of femininist criticism that a real women's literature must kill the "angel in the house." In fact, as long as any fiction achieves resolution by killing off characters—"angels" *or* "monsters"—it is a romantic fiction.[40]

As Frye says, "at its most naive, 'the romance' is an endless form in which a central character who never develops or ages goes through one adventure after another," unless it is given the literary form of the quest. In this form the hero passes through "a point of ritual death" before his "exaltation."[41] In the fiction we will examine, the heroine may indeed be on a quest, pass through a point of ritual death (periods of amnesia or insanity or being cast, bound hand and foot, into a dungeon are common), and she may be "exalted"—for that is how she regards coming into her rightful inheritance and/or accepting her true love's proposal of marriage. Yet her character cannot change. In other words, the central figure in these books is really no more complete or significant than the others, for they all play out her inner drama, in the disguise of semirealistic dress.

Each story derives, then, its interest from the accuracy with which it replicates usually unconscious emotional processes. Repressed fantasies, when brought into consciousness, can bring with them for the moment a sense of great personal freedom and power, of a "reality" beyond the everyday. This is one reason that the characters are not portrayed as responsible for their actions, except in the most simple black and white terms. It is also why the settings of these novels are as significant as the characters.[42] For example, houses, cottages, castles, Egyptian tombs and others, attics, basements, and underground passages are the focus or source of a spectrum of emotional reactions, from terror and loathing through longing (hopeless and hopeful) to a melting satisfaction. This aspect of physical setting is often, even usually, a metaphor for the female body itself.[43] This fascination with the house image remains a constant in these stories, though it will require separate, different treatment in each historical period.

Like the tragic hero, the heroine of romance cannot know herself. The popular romance plot is resolved by an apparent affirmation of social (and economic) order, because a heroine at the center of any of these stories cannot even develop the qualities necessary to threaten that order—as a hero may do.[44] Despite the fact that her story is played out on an inner stage, she is relentlessly portrayed as impeded at every turn by her inability—to make a living wage without paying for it, to lose her culturally valued innocence in time to avoid seduction and/or abandonment, to choose whether or not to marry (let alone bear children), to survive the rupture of family ties—or even, usually, to consciously imagine any of these unconventional behaviors. This is the other reason she is not responsible for her actions. The rigidities of the irrational within us mirror the irrational without.

The four chapters that follow deal with a variety of women's books. Chapter Two is about the sentimental gothic novel that was popular in the United States in the early national period. Chapter Three examines the literature of the "cult of domesticity" that flourished in the middle years of the 19th century. Chapter Four analyzes a number of different sorts of romantic fiction, written during the period in which the United States entered the 20th century and took part in two World Wars. Chapter Five is about the genre of women's fiction that began its rise to popularity in the 1950s, the "new gothic," or story of romantic suspense.

The scope and complexity of the subject matter defies any attempt to impose a theory of continuous development. The historical transformations in question—of family structures and of fictional structures—reflect each other without suggesting a pattern of linear evolution. In Chapter Two, an essentially European genre is used in America to contain the terrors of change. In Chapter Three, these terrors are controlled within a native form, the domestic novel. In Chapter Four the variety of fiction dealt with reflects, I believe, the variety of strategies with which women of that time attempted to actually *confront* terrors that commanded attention without quite defeating them. The renascence of coherent literary genres of women's popular fiction in the 1950s and after may be explicable in terms of the overwhelming nature of more recent terrors; certainly these genres face, most resolutely of all, straight away from contemporary historical realities.

Whatever our view ought to be of how these books are historically determined, their inner world of fantasy is demonstrably not constructed from conflicts with the patriarchial capitalist–industrial world. It is, rather, made up of the symbols and images of pre-oedipal mother–child relation and the attempt to outgrow these. In other words, women have not written "escape" fiction for other women all these years in an effort, conscious or unconscious, to subvert the forms of male domination. It is, rather, the far more powerful domination of the whole self by parts of the self which has been read and written about.

That domination is the door by which the heroine enters the dark house of romance.

2

LEAVING THE ROOF:
The Early National Period

I. The Period

During the years between the Revolutionary War and 1830, geo-
graphical and economic dislocations were the common experience
of American families. The turmoil of the Revolutionary period was
followed by commercial and westward expansion, the growth of
urban areas, and the beginning of industrialization. One historian,
indeed, comments that in this period the change in women's experience outran, in pace and intensity, changes for more than a century
before and after.[45] The word "independence" began to take on
economic and personal as well as political meaning. The decreasing
availability of farmland close to "home" as well as the factory system encouraged autonomy from the original household economy.[46]
Children might no longer be around to be old-age insurance for
their parents, nor earn the same sort of living their parents had,
nor take the traditional attitude toward them.[47] However, the rearing of daughters continued to be different from the rearing of sons.
While writers on the role of the Republican mother assured her
that she might best participate in civil culture by rearing independent and self-reliant sons, her daughters were to be reared to
replicate her own function.[48]

When, in the English middle class of the 18th century, the closed
domesticated nuclear family had begun to appear, its most salient
characteristic had been an increased interest in child-rearing *by the*

mother. In America, this development took place only toward the end of the 18th century.[49] An expanding literature on various aspects of women's lives, British and American, stressed an increase in the amount of attention to be paid by mothers to their small children. By the turn of the century, mothers, not fathers, were the primary targets of advice, in books and magazines, on the moral upbringing and education of older sons and daughters. This higher evaluation of motherhood nevertheless implied a new, exclusive preoccupation with its duties.[50] One writer has written of this period as the beginning of the "emancipation of the American child."[51] Certainly a new recognition of children's special needs began to extend the time of life in which boys and girls enjoyed a new freedom from restraint and responsibility. The freedom enjoyed by their mothers under these circumstances is another question.

Possibly because of the period's social disequilibrium, and current anxieties over the country's moral standards and stability, American maternal responsibilities quickly became formulated in far more dramatic terms than even those of Victorian England. Though some middle-class women worked outside the home (especially before marriage),[52] this was considered justifiable only on the grounds of economic necessity. Woman's true moral responsibility was to the private, domestic sphere of society. The public sphere of politics and business—impersonal, highly competitive and taxing of human energies— was the *male* sphere. And in order to operate effectively there, to support his family, the aspiring capitalist husband and father must be able to come home to a secluded spot where feelings could be cultivated and indulged, and where comfort, ease, and other finer things of life were arranged for by the women of the household.

Of course this ideal, in the period in question, could only be realized at the apex of the social order. Yet to the degree that a wife had leisure at all, she was supposed to use it for the creation of the ideal home, and for the physical, mental, moral, and spiritual welfare of her husband and children.[53] Economic man in 19th century America went in peril of his soul: Woman stayed home from the marketplace to save it, and to save his children—most especially the daughters, who were to carry on this work, whose roles "shaded imperceptibly and ineluctably" into this exaltation of the maternal role.[54] When a boy in early 19th century America accepted his social definition as a man, he took on the task of supporting himself, and also a family. In the way he did this, he was allowed, indeed expected, to compete with his father. When a girl became a woman, she was not to compete with her mother; her task was to replicate her. Woman's role allowed far fewer variations than man's.

Here, in this ideal English and American home, mothers and daughters fostered an atmosphere of sensibility: in America, a specifically religious sensibility. Popular literature helped. Women had been given—since 1740, when *Clarissa* was published—feminine heroines of romantic fiction whose social and economic value *was* their unworldly purity. A marriage of choice, for love, was their destiny and reason for being. According to at least one historian, romantic love itself was "a product . . . of learned cultural expectations, which became fashionable in the late 18th century thanks largely to the spread of novel reading."[55] Well before the Revolution, British sentimental novels of seduction were widely consumed by the American middle-class wife and daughter, and their popularity was intensified after the Revolution.[56] It is no surprise to find that one-third of the books produced by American authors between 1779 and 1829 were "written for or by women. In subject, form and characterization they followed British models."[57] Small wonder, either, that the sentimental novel with the seduction plot, which indicated that a young woman had no worth of her own, "no choices in life between marriage and death,"[58] was popular in novels imported from abroad, and in those that began finally to appear in America in the last decade of the 18th century.[59] Of the texts covered in this chapter, all published or sold in America before 1830, half are British in origin. These British and American productions are almost indistinguishable, though this will begin to change as early as 1840. Nevertheless, the influence of the British images of women purveyed in this sort of fiction remains important.

Like their British counterparts, American moralists recognized and deplored the fantastic nature of popular fiction, decrying the "passion for novels" as dangerous; as one put it, they "hold up *life*, it is true, but it is not as yet *life* in America."[60] In part, such criticism reflects the Republican objection to the fashionable parasitism of upper-class women.[61] Yet many of the novels discussed in this book mount their own attack on fashion and even on material wealth, as we will see. Both the criticism and the fiction mark the transition to woman's new role as the nonmaterialistic half of society. The fear that she will be corrupted surfaces with increasing regularity in the writings of this time.

Here is a slightly later American critic's description of popular women's fiction:

> If . . . [a novel] present an untrue picture of life, it imparts false and exaggerated notions which are sure to corrupt the heart . . . it tends to fill young minds with fancies and expectations which can never, in the natural course of things, be gratified or accomplished. It presents a double picture of the human condition; one a paradise, the other a hell . . .[62]

This is a formal description of a romance—except, perhaps, the intention to corrupt the heart. In fact, the fiction of the period departs widely from the rules for romance (as opposed to the novel, which deals with the realities of the external rather than the internal world), by discussing at length "women's status with advice as to their behavior and training. This material form[s] no integral part of the plots."[63] The intention of this material is, clearly, to *train* the heart, since women are no longer supposed to train any other important faculties.[64] The plots and characterizations of these stories also reveal much about the new ideology of the era. Heroine and hero, devil and angel in the house, mother and child crowd these pages, enacting—on one level—precisely what the society expected of its ideal types.

Yet on another level we will find what I like to call the rebellion of the heart: a release of the socially unacceptable energies and imageries of the inner world. Side by side with a detailed prescription for "true womanhood"[65] we will find a bitter indictment and a profound fear of it. These books, and those which follow in their tradition, reached—and reach—the mass of women for whom marriage is a loss of freedom they must choose.[66] In lurid detail, these books show what they openly admitted about their feelings, and what they had to disguise. Girls, wives, mothers—they began a new genre, incorporating elements of the gothic novel, the sentimental novel, and even, as we will see, the old-style romance. These forms have in common one emotional tone: a persistent vague terror, attached to a number of even vaguer objects.

II. The Fiction

What were the women really afraid of? I can begin to answer this question by a discussion of two texts unlike any of the others, two quite conscious satires on the old romance form, popular before Richardson, in which the heroine miraculously escapes various perils, and is mechanically rewarded by marriage to wealth and a title.[67] (In none of the other stories I will be examining, does the heroine escape peril, and if a reward is provided her, though it may be marriage, it will be to a good bourgeois. In novels by American women, noble lineage and great wealth are *per se* evidence of incurable frivolity, or downright corruption.)

The first of these two satirical productions was Charlotte Lennox's *The Female Quixote* (1752), an Englishwoman's straightforward attack on the fictional fare of the earlier half of the century, which was well received by the reading public; it continued to be published until 1820, and was praised by Johnson, Richardson, and Fielding. Charlotte Lennox made her living by writing, after an "unfortunate marriage"—but she ended her days "in penury."[68] The heroine, Arabella, has undergone a gross distortion of her naturally good intellectual powers, by being allowed to read bad translations of French romances, and not much else, during her formative years. Her mother, who might have prevented this, died when she was born. (This pattern will recur.) As a consequence of her reading, Arabella believes that "Love [is] the ruling Principle of the World; that every other Passion [is] subordinate to this." Therefore she interprets each slightest action of any male with whom she comes in contact as evidence of his Passion for her: "She had such a strange Facility in reconciling every Incident to her Own fantastick Ideas, that every new Object added Strength to the fatal Deception she laboured under." Threatened forced marriage, abduction, rape, and incest, not to mention such milder insults as a lover's despairing suicide at her very feet, obsess her continuously, and render her entirely unable to perceive social reality: A gardener is an enamoured Unknown in disguise; a prostitute, a maiden in distress, and so on. In other words, Arabella lives in a world made up of her own projected sexual fantasies, and anticipates at any moment being ravished away into a country "far distant from [her] own." At the novel's end, after she has passed through an almost-fatal illness (another recurrent element of plot), a preacher is finally able to convince her that her "Terrors and Suspicions" have no basis in fact. "He cannot carry you to any of these dreadful Places, because there is no such Castle, Desert, Cavern or Lake," says he. Her eyes opened, Arabella promises to try to be a worthy wife to the husband her father chooses for her.

Despite her grasp on what was silly about the old-fashioned genre, Miss Lennox subsequently went on to produce novels without a shred of satiric purpose, containing all the old-style clichés that could be imported into the sentimental novel of the later part of the century.

An American novel in the satirical mode, almost certainly influenced by Lennox's book, is Tabitha Tenney's *Female Quixotism, or the Extravagant Adventures of Dorcasina Sheldon*. Tabitha Tenney was born in New Hampshire in 1762 and lived in Washington several winters after 1800, when her husband was a member of Congress. Her own education was at her mother's hands, her father having died in her infancy, and on the literary side consisted of "a few well chosen books."[69] The book was first published in 1829, and is a far harsher and saltier treatment of the old-fashioned romance—for one thing, this heroine's desires are not merely projected; they are also acted out. Dorcas, also early orphaned and indulged in novel-reading by her father, is *not* beautiful; rather, "middling" in looks. At the age of 18 she assumes the name of Dorcasina and embarks on the career of romantic heroine— unfortunately, in her case, there is no one around she can imagine as her hero. She becomes 24, then 34, before even an unscrupulous Irish adventurer attempts her, and she is disabused with extreme difficulty of her illusions regarding him. (Gentle words won't break into this fantasy world; she must see him disgraced and flogged before his regiment!)

The typical situation of a young officer, wounded and brought to recover at the family home, follows. Dorcasina is duped by his manservant, in disguise as his master, into an elopement. When he reveals himself, she runs home, and is cured for a few more years. But at the age of 60 or so, after an interlude concerned with the death of her father, her own grief, and consequent illness, she falls in love with a servant posing as a gentleman. This time her friends must intervene, using money and a staged false kidnapping, to protect and undeceive her. The story concludes with her own rousing warning against the reading of romances. Tenney apparently experienced the same difficulty as Lennox, in attempting to emphasize the values of mind over those of the heart in a social milieu moving rapidly toward Romanticism— she wrote no more fiction at all.

There is much in this sort of plot, however parodied in these two cases, that is repeated in the nonsatirical fiction of the period. The motherless state of the girl motivates the attempt and near-success of the deceitful male, and even the good man is untrustworthy. (In *Dorcasina*, her friend marries a good man, for love, and reports most unfavorably on the first year of marriage, while Arabella's husband is irascible, to say the least.) These twin themes, the young woman protected by no or poor mothering, and the duplicity of men, are to be met with again and again in the women's fiction of the years between our two satirical examples. They are, I think, two sides of the same coin. In Lennox's and Tenney's books, it is the whole point that the heroine's self-deceptions exceed whatever is in fact practiced on them.

III. The Absent Mother

By the time Tenney wrote, American women were becoming familiar with the notion that their time and emotional energy were naturally to be spent on childcare. It is therefore the absence of a mother's guiding example, "educating her girls entirely at home . . . unrepiningly dedicating the best part of her life to solitude, tender maternal cares, vigilant attention, and incessant anxiety" (*Clarentine*), that permits the grossly mistaken view of life of these heroines. In this way, the theme of maternal deprivation enters the fiction on a conscious level. Something is sure to be wrong with a daughter who has not had the benefit of a mother's care.

However, the dire consequences of this lack also enter the fiction in the disguises of unconscious infantile fantasy projections. According to Kernberg, two developmental tasks are accomplished together in the first year of life, if they are accomplished at all. Before the infant is able to differentiate self-representation from representations of the other, she has differentiated a pleasurable presence (which is rewarding) from a painful one (which punishes). The former "unit," the nucleus of eventual good representations of mother and self, will provide a child with the ability to trust, both self and other, and also the ability to recognize the other. Trust and recognition are inseparable developmental tasks, which can be interfered with if the mother is absent or somehow unreliable.[70]

Melanie Klein further clarifies the psychological picture we can compare to our stereotyped fictional characters, morally blind girls and their treacherous love objects. To inadequate mothering, at the stage described above, the child will respond with the defense mechanisms of splitting and projection. Both are attempts to ward off destruction with dissociation of the painful, and both may lead (at an unconscious level in later life) to a perceived "threat of annihilation by persecutors." The leading anxiety here is that the persecutor will get inside you![71] Thus the "bad" mother representation is converted into the fictional character of a seducer who will also—very predictably—abandon the heroine.

What more is implied by this persistently absent fictional mother? What experiences may have led the writers of these stories to cling to this convention, and to the emotional climate, of orphan heroine? Were they, and their readers, in some sense motherless? Charlotte Smith's mother, for example, died when Charlotte was three. Yet the incidence of maternal death was no higher during these decades than it had ever been. The emotional significance of the family, in an unstable society, was greater, as was the opportunity of the middle-class woman to elaborate on her feelings.[72] In the early months of life, *magic denial* is another common defense. If one fears annihilation by persecutors (if one's mother is experiencing a shift in social status and social expectations, that leaves her uneasy, smothering, anxious, repressed), one simply fantasizes their annihilation.[73] If it works, the fantasy persists at some level into adult life. With what ultimate consequences, these fictions may perhaps show us.

Other targets in Tenney's story will crop up again in this and later chapters: the attempt at a forced marriage, mourning the death of a parent (in fact, Tenney gives this a long and serious treatment, which gives us some idea of the new emphasis this plot element is to receive), abduction and imprisonment, a vulnerable, sensitive, weak hero. For the moment, however, let us trace the other two themes, that of the motherless heroine, and that of the duplicity of men, through a collection of fictions published or sold in America before 1820.

In 10 of the 14 texts I will be discussing, the heroine is early bereft of her mother and in four cases (*Emmeline, Clarentine, The Hapless Orphan,* and *Constantia*), totally orphaned. (Actually, Constantia meets her long-lost father toward the end of that novel, but he dies while she's finding out who he is.) Two other heroines, Louisa and Rosalie (of *Montalbert*), find long-lost mothers from whom they were separated in early childhood by unavoidable accidents. Such reunions are so affecting that the mother in each case loses consciousness. Rosalie has begun to love her mother dearly even before the moment of revelation: "Were I her daughter, I think it would be the greatest happiness of my life to watch her very wishes before she could express them . . . ", she writes to a friend. And after the discovery, their hours together are their greatest emotional indulgence, although Rosalie is quite newly wed at the time. Separated from husband and mother, later in the story, for this young woman, "even the passionate fondness she felt for her child most forcibly recalled that affection which she owed her mother."

For Louisa, the discovery that a woman she is already learning to regard and obey as a mother *is* her mother provokes rapture: "Oh, joy! oh, happiness," said Louisa, sinking at Mrs. Belmont's feet, "I have a mother—and such a mother—Bless, bless your enraptured daughter!" Even Clarentine goes into "transports" over the discovery of a genuine aunt. It must be remembered that New England children of the day were expected to evince enormous devotion and gratitude toward their parents, and to make them happy in any way they could.[74] Such socially appropriate behavior did not, however, entail emotional excesses—on the contrary, children were expected to be meek and modest in their parents' presence. But "transports" are to be expected, when the early developmental process from symbiosis to individuation has been interrupted or blocked. It is the rule for the heroines of these fictions to enact this developmental flaw and its repercussions in opposing extremes of feeling. The good behavior of a dutiful daughter, then, is more than fully dramatized in these stories. Yet this acceptable message appears side by side with violently unacceptable images of fear and loathing of mothers. The emotional seesaw between oceanic bliss and paranoid suspicion is further dramatized by the appearance of characters representing the bad mother, often in the same story with a good one.

The curse of a bad mother befalls Eliza, Adeline, Laura (in *Self Control*), and Rosalie. Eliza's mother is described as proud, cold, and unloving toward her older daughter. She attempts to force her into a marriage with a man she does not love, in order to finance a younger and beloved sister's love match. "Cruel mother," Eliza's lover remarks, and Eliza meekly replies that her mother "must needs sacrifice the happiness of one of her daughters—how natural too, that it must be she who is least dear to her." The lovers part, and Eliza marries her mother's choice, planning to do her duty by all: "only learn to make others happy." The novel is a case study in self-sacrifice, and Eliza's own daughter is described on the last page as follows: "The virtues of the mother, were hereditary in the daughter, who in like manner directed them towards promoting the happiness of her fellow creatures."

Rosalie's adoptive mother tries the same thing: "I am thus to be dressed up, and offered like an animal to sale; and my mother seems to think it a matter of course . . . " Rosalie cries. Not only does Rosalie—alone among the heroines of this chapter—openly express "anger and resentment," she actually escapes by eloping with her lover. The penalties that are exacted from her before novel's end are, however, uniquely dire. Laura, in the novel promisingly titled *Self Control*, had a mother who tried to bring her up as the opposite of her "natural self," with "blows, disgraces, and deprivations." This mother is, however, granted a months-long deathbed attendance at the story's outset, and throughout the story Laura's capacity for self-blame exceeds that for self-control. By her mother's callous treatment of her, she is driven to the refuge of her imagination (portrayed, of course, as unsafe, in all of these novels), and her imagination creates for her a totally false image of an officer, Col. Hargrave, which takes her 200 pages to correct. This course of events, which we saw parodied in the satirical novels, recurs regularly in the novels of this period. Any undisciplined course of reading (in the absence of a mother who prevents it) will set it off.

An especially intriguing variation is that offered by the childhood experience and first love of Adeline Mowbray, in Opie's novel of that name. In this English writer's fictionalized account of Mary Wollstonecraft's life, her didactic purpose is clear. (Opie did not need to support herself by her writing, and her last years she spent in retirement, after becoming a Quaker.) Adeline's mother, because of her parents' "blind folly," had been allowed to indulge her bent for reading "abstruse systems of morals and metaphysics, or new theories in politics," quite "left to the decisions of her own inexperienced enthusiasm." This mother, although the education of her daughter has been sadly neglected, and contradictory when pursued, is nevertheless respected by her daughter for her abilities and even earns her "most devoted attachment" because she has (once) nursed her child through a long and serious illness. This doesn't seem sufficient real cause for devotion, obviously. For the psychological motivation that convinces the reader in such cases, we must assume a persisting infantile fantasy of a perfectly good and loving mother, split off from the bad one, and endlessly, if hopelessly, longed for. This fantasy, aroused by young women's unhappy early experiences, and projected onto their lovers, accounts for the persistence of their attachments, and their repercussions, as we shall see.

As Jung says, "Separation from the mother is sufficient only if the archetype is included."[75] It is not enough to run away from one's own individual mother (as Adeline eventually does); one must also have the opportunity to progress beyond the intense unconscious attachment to the Great Mother archetype. A "bad" or absent mother does not allow this archetype to be consciously activated and outgrown.

Adeline sets out to master her mother's theoretical knowledge and to put it into practice, too. This maneuver[76] might serve her very well, if the author of the book on free love which she reads did not turn out to be "young and handsome too!" The consequences are predictable, but in fact Adeline does not elope with him until her situation at home is made impossible by the sexual advances of her mother's new husband (which Adeline resents most on her mother's behalf—so that she cannot bear to complain of them). Once she has fled with Glenmurray, however, he makes her an offer of marriage.

On principle, she refuses it, and he dies, eventually, of the nervous tension her stubbornness induces. Her grief, like her principled action, seems violently sincere, but a certain unconscious generalized vengefulness toward the beloved "protector" figure cannot be ignored. Moreover, her grief over Glenmurray's death pales beside her grief at her mother's continued refusal to see her or forgive her for the elopement. "Even while leaning on the shoulder of her lover, she sighed to be once more clasped to the bosom of her mother." Adeline has her only attack of hysterics upon hearing that her mother "detests" her: "with a frantic scream [she] kept repeating the words, 'she detests me!' till . . . she sunk, sobbing convulsively, exhausted on the bed to which they carried her."

It appears to be possible, in this fictional world, to develop a friendship with a suitable older woman, in order to mitigate some of the worst results of bad or absent mothers.[77] But this is not certain: Laura, for example, has a surrogate mother in Mrs. Douglas, the clergyman's wife, and still loves imprudently; nor can Constantia's foster parents prevent her from inappropriately loving a chevalier. In fact, Constantia apparently receives a more persuasive, though still vain, warning in a somewhat occult fashion. When waiting to meet her lover in a ruined cottage, she falls into a troubled contemplation of a long length of "rich auburn hair . . . the melancholy memorial of life;—the painful vacuum—the affecting desolation of a scene that presents every dear and familiar object, except that one which vivified and embellished all!" Chastened in mood by this (as she later discovers), her mother's hair, she attempts to leave. It is too late; she is locked in, and abduction by her enemies promptly follows.

In any case, good mother surrogates are not easy to find. Rather, these stories swarm with wicked ones of all sorts, responsible for as much destruction as the seducers, brutal rakes, heartless officers, compulsive gamblers, and mere degenerate weaklings who constitute the bad men of the stories. And the heroines are equally if not more prone to be deceived by the women. Again, real stepmothers were, then as now, a usual experience, though death rather than divorce provided them. Smith, for example, was forced into her disastrous marriage by her stepmother when only 15.[78]

In a chapter of Charlotte Temple[79] entitled "French teachers not always the best women in the world," we meet a prototype of the deceiving woman, Mlle. La Rue, whose "spirit of intrigue" causes her to coerce Charlotte into a meeting with the man who is to seduce and abandon her. So obdurate is the viciousness of La Rue that only after seven subsequent years of "riot, dissipation and vice," leading to "poverty and sickness," does she realize the horror of her ways and comment that her "vile arts blasted . . . a fair bud of innocence . . . ere it was half blown."

The evil aunt in The Hapless Orphan, an American text, is less a problem to Caroline than is another young woman, Eliza, whose lover has committed suicide for love of Caroline. The rest of the book details Eliza's revenge, and the various disasters that overcome Caroline's friends. "I seem to make wretched every family in which I reside!" she comments at one point. (This claim is also made by Louisa, *The Lovely Orphan*.) Eliza spreads calumnies that estrange Caroline's lover, and he dies in battle alienated from her.

Eliza is not, of course, a representation of the bad mother, but rather of the bad self-representation attached to it. For years, literary criticism has been satisfied to comment on the presence of angel and devil women in European and American literature. Their 19th century forms, in which the blonde is self-sacrificing to the point of self-extinction, and the brunette is both morally and physically rapacious, are especially extreme. The dichotomy is usually explained (if it is explained) as a result of Victorian masculine psychological defense mechanisms, or at least hypocrisy.[80] Clearly the prevailing masculine ideology did specify purity, religiosity, and docility in its potential wives and mothers. But then, so did mothers anxiously seek to instill these qualities, or the appearance of them, in their daughters, in order to fit them for the "only life possible"—one like their own. The psychological mechanisms in question are indeed prescribed by the culture, but begin their development even before socialization takes place. A female infant learns she is good if she is quiet and clean; bad if she is noisy, dirty, greedy. What happens to impulses toward these latter qualities? In Jungian terms, they are cast into the shadow—and Eliza is Caroline's negative shadow, that hostile outsider, "accursed, alienated," which the lack of an adequate experience of mother love can produce.[81]

So, in the fantasy world of this and the other novels, psychic reality is split into several characters, and Caroline cannot recognize Eliza as a shadow projection; instead, she abets her destructive behavior and unwittingly helps her enemy by her persistent self-blame and passivity. She eventually acquires another (but dull) suitor, only to be abducted by two highwaymen in Eliza's pay. We last hear of her from two young physicians, as an interesting cadaver. At last, this character has gotten the punishment she wanted.

In *Clarentine*, old Mrs. Harrington is also a malicious rumor monger, and compounds an already desperate situation: Clarentine is "an alien, without any natural friends and assured support" in the Delmington home, where her love for the son, Edgar, has incurred his mother's enmity. Clarentine sensibly transfers her affection to Somerset—but a Mrs. Hertford is after him, plotting to make him believe there are grounds for jealousy. The whole matter takes 200 pages to unravel. These shadow characters reliably either tempt to, indulge in, or spread lies about, illicit sexual behavior: A young woman's "enemies" can be counted on for that.

In *Self Control*, Laura Montreville must live with her aunt, Lady Pelham, who aids the male "persecutor" who has already, by the middle of Volume

Two, brought Laura to the condition of "the land where the Whirlwind has passed; dreary and desolate" and filled with humiliation and shame at her folly. The obstinate persecution nevertheless continues until the novel's final page, when the villain finally confesses to her *true* lover that despite all appearances to the contrary, she remains an angel (read virgin). This combination, or doubling, of a bad mother figure and a persecutory lover, in league with each other, is as persistent a motif as their opposite numbers. The fundamental similarity between the relationship to mother and to the men in these heroine's lives is nowhere more clearly illustrated. These two together nearly kill Laura; what saves her, apparently, where others perish, is her eventual ability to see through her ideal images of them; one step, at least, toward selfhood. The form of the fiction, of course, precludes the taking of the next step. She cannot make her shadow a part of herself, any more than she can fuse the two maternal images, or the exciting with the proper suitor.

In *Amelia, or Malevolence Defeated*, the malevolent character is again the embittered and envious older woman, who adores blasting young love. However this fiend is thwarted, and "falls into a rapid decline" after the wedding her "passion for mischief" could not prevent. Death is simply the only way that the bad mother, the shadow, and the villain can effectively be dealt with in these stories.

In *Emmeline*, a similar "odious and hateful envy . . . [has] ulcerated" the minds of a Mrs. Ashwood and a shadowy Miss Galton, who seek to defame the heroine in the eyes of her wealthy and weak lover, whose "heart so full of sensibility" renders him credulous to their calumies. The whole scandalous story of the birth of an illegitimate child is successfully maintained by these confederates for another 100 pages, with misunderstandings and mysterious repercussions for still another 100.

IV. The Duplicity of Men

The confusion of all these heroines about whether men can or cannot be trusted is a persistent theme. Seduction or abduction of the principal character occurs in nine of these texts (and of subsidiary characters, in four); in eight, with fatal results—death, described in lingering detail, in childbed and/or of "brainfever." This particular narrative pattern is much less common in American fiction after 1820; as one critic points out, after 1820, American women writers were in reaction against the Richardsonian vision of women as sexual prey.[82] Yet the interwoven plot device that remains a constant to the present day is the heroine's anxious and stubborn inability to trust men enough to tell a good one from a bad one. Instead, she is compelled to delude herself into dependence on an undependable one; this dilemma and its results preoccupy nine of the heroines discussed in this book.

I have already partly described the difficulties of Laura, in *Self Control*. Like other heroines in this state of confusion, she is prone to moods of intense remorse and self-disgust. Once free of her infatuation with the persecutory Hargrave, she must inform her true-love that she is unworthy of him: "I wish you had known me ere the serpent wound me in his poisoned coils," she declares, and later insists on releasing him from their engagement because she imagines herself dishonored. Laura's very poor self-image, then, is typically involved with her fantasy image of that other who has had most power over her, her "rejecting" mother—and the heartless seducer to whom she had temporarily transferred her infantile longings for love as "ideal perfection," and who rejected her, in reality.

An emotional revulsion into extreme self-loathing after being disillusioned about a lover also appears strongly in *The Coquette*, where the ruined daughter, assured of her (unsuspecting) mother's love, "struggled from her embrace, and looking at her with wild despair, exclaimed, 'this is too much. Oh, this unmerited goodness is more than I can bear!'" She elopes, "to avoid what she has never experienced, and feels herself unable to support, a mother's frown . . . the heartrending sight of a parent's grief!" As in the case of Adeline Mowbray, the hope of her mother's forgiveness is her only solace, but the fear of maternal disapproval far outweighs that hope. Similarly, during Charlotte Temple's last illness, her hallucinations are of mother: "Oh, could you see the horrid sight which I now behold—there—stands my dear mother, her poor bosom bleeding at every vein, her gentle, affectionate heart torn in a thousand places, and all for the loss of a ruined, ungrateful child. Save me—save me—from her frown."

These bouts of compunction are not undergone only on a mother' behalf; for example, in Opie's *Father and Daughter*, Agnes devotes her life to tending for the father she has driven mad by running off with a man. She even dies when he does. (Again, it is worthwhile to point out that tending a dying parent was a common real life experience among these authors and readers—Anna Seward, for example, "nursed her father through his slow decay."[83]) These young women also suffer considerably for their rejected suitors. Caroline's monument to her estranged lover Evremont is a case in point, cupids, willows, inscription, and all. In view of the trouble they have caused the young women, the concern that Clarentine shows for her weak suitor Edgar, and Emmeline's for the ineffectual Delamere, seem excessive. Eliza allows the visits of her first love, Herman, only after she is sure of her indissoluble oneness with her husband—and her son, named after Herman, promptly dies.

This literally fatal inability to extricate themselves from moral confusion is elaborated metaphorically in every story by the mental and physical debility that accompany it. Emmeline, upon being abducted by Delamere, feeling herself at fault, falls prey to an "unspecified fever," causing him to "repent of his wild attempt." The ravages of her extreme anxiety shame him into taking her back intact, rather than any show she makes of moral strength. Such moral strength as she possesses is, typically, turned against herself, in guilt and self-reproach. Laura is similarly affected by the "violence" of Hargrave's attentions (she is also at this point in the story giving her father nearly all the food they can afford to buy), so that her true love is "shocked at the paleness and dejection of her altered countenance." Of course she does not complain, or explain. Rosalie, in *Montalbert*, is unconscious for two hours when her lover leaves her in Italy, and loses her mind completely when he sends for their child, and men "force . . . the child from the convulsive grasp of its apparently dying mother." She does not, in fact, recover until the boy is returned to her. In at least one case, that of the Lady Adeline in *Emmeline*, childbirth cures a suicidal depression that has lasted for 100 pages. It is more usual, however, for these young women (for example, the Coquette, Charlotte Temple, and Amelia) to fail to survive their lying-in. Of course, where the child dies, as it does in four of these books, the mother dies too or is insane for months.

The paths of those heroines who summon up some physical endurance are not smooth. The moral imperative (addressed to Agnes when she is suicidal) "Unnatural mother! would you forsake your child?" would bear really very little weight if the mother could not arrange to suffer while surviving. Having decided to live, Agnes informs her old nurse's daughter that "it would be presumption in any woman who has quitted the path of virtue to intrude herself, however high her rank might be, on the meanest of her acquaintance whose honour is spotless," and she goes to work as a nurse at the local insane asylum. Similarly, Constantia can soothe the "widowed" heart she is left with by her father's death only by assuaging the grief of others; Laura, after her father's death, decides that only life's "useful" ends are left to her; and the repentant Dorcas ends her days living a life of benevolence.

None live for themselves, but only in terms of a complicated arrangement of projections: Need and fear and rage are all attributed to others, and these others must be watched over and cared for, protected from themselves and other horrors, and propitiated. Klein describes, for example, how we play simultaneously the roles of loving parents and loving children in order to make everything "all right."[84] A vast amount of anxious benevolence is to be expected of the otherwise restricted lives portrayed in this body of fiction.

These guilt-stricken heroines are also frequently grief-stricken. The melodramatic quality with which grief is described in these books is notorious. Can "exhausted nature sustain so severe a stroke?" (*The Hapless Orphan*). "For six months her frenzy resisted all the efforts of medicine" (*Adeline Mowbray*). The overwhelming guilt feelings that characterize an incomplete work of mourning are described again and again in the stories: The heroines all feel they have failed their parents or protectors, with an intensity that is not sufficiently explained by their violation of social expectations. The suggestion is very strong that beneath this conscious reason for sorrow there lies the unconscious fear—and consequent fear of punishment—that their repressed infantile rage was the cause of death.

Mrs. River (who miscarried when her husband died) always felt "unworthy" of the marriage; Adeline actually accuses herself of killing her husband. Their sense of being abandoned by the death of the other is portrayed with a passion which points directly to the probable source of this theme's popular appeal. Here, for example, is Emmeline's estimate of her situation: "She considered herself as a being belonging to nobody; as having no right to claim the protection of anyone; no power to procure for herself the necessaries of life . . . she was terrified at the prospect before her." Feeling that they now belong to nobody, are unprotected, unable to care for themselves, and feeling once more the infant's rage at this condition, these heroines unleash the self-destructive intensity of their grief, until nature calls a halt and "the pearly drop is petrified" (*The Hapless Orphan*). This guilty terror of abandonment is of course at the core of the inability to tell whether another person is good or bad, and of the inability to trust her—or him.

V. The Dependent Self

A similarity to the life patterns of those who read this fiction is easy to see. They were encouraged or forced to depend economically and for their sense of self on others, and to pay for this in "loving" service. In fact, unmarried women had realistic cause to believe they could not be self-supporting.[85] If they were daughters of mothers who were attempting to find their life's satisfaction in child-rearing, they learned, as early as it is possible to learn (and repress) anything, that they could never satisfy the demands for total emotional gratification that were placed upon them, never be "good" enough, to anyone. Moreover, imprisoned as they were within these restrictive roles, girl children and young women also found themselves inhabitants of female bodies; the implications of this fact, as they dawned gradually on young women at the turn of the 19th century, most likely provoked both conscious and unconscious fears and resentments. The female body's invisibilities, when the culture dictates that they are unmentionable, can foster fantasies of an inside full of badness. The major gothic image, of the imprisoning and threatening house, is at once an image of self and of the mother who put one there.[86]

What happens if a young women *does* show anger about all this? We have only one example of a girl's expressed resentment in all these books, Rosalie's, and it is Rosalie who is held for months in a gloomy fortress in Naples, the longest period of incarceration in a set of stories where imprisonment is as regular a feature as flight, broken families, or elopement. In Rosalie's case imprisonment is accepted with resignation; in others it is clearly self-imposed.

Constantia, for example, is abducted and imprisoned in an evil marquis' chateau. She finds a key, and attempts an escape down a dark hallway lined with sculptures: "Maimed and gigantic figures . . . seemed starting with wild and distorted attitudes . . . into preternatural animation." She passes through a "dreary and desolate" chapel, and arrives eventually in a dungeon, containing a stone coffin and a "meagre and ghastly figure," a madman, who tells her his story. Shaken, she goes back up to her room, and leaves again only when the chateau is abandoned because of the (French Revolutionary) War. Then she visists him in the dungeon again, observing that "the apartment, though not humid, was cold enough to communicate a shiver to beings who know what it is to enjoy the fireside comforts: the cheerful hearth, so justly alotted to the household gods, and within whose magic circle a thousand graceful affections and nameless courtesies seem to dwell!"

The explanation for this odd interpolation is very simple. This poor madman is not only the true marquis, but Constantia's real father; the pathos is unutterably intense, for Constantia, like Charlotte, Adeline, Agnes, the Coquette, Rosalie, Amelia, and a number of supernumerary characters, has taken a step outside the "magic circle" of the home, and will not be allowed the reconciliation with parents, which alone can fully atone for that act.

Only the direst of threats, only the total assurance of some other respectable protection, can begin to justify the step outside the home—and even these may not suffice. Adeline cannot leave until her stepfather has attempted to rape her: "What will become of me! . . . my mother's roof is no longer a protection to me . . . whither can I go, and where can I seek for refuge?" She flees to her lover Glenmurray: "Oh! I am safe now! . . . I come to seek shelter in your arms from misery and dishonor." But she has left the frying pan for the fire, and the pain of the decision is incurable. At this novel's end, her reconciliation with her mother complete, Adeline has not left off regretting her step outside: "I am assured of your love again, and I have not a want beside. Still, I could like, I could wish to be once more under a *parent's roof!*"

Other heroines end up even less luckily, "wandering, an exile," (*The Gamesters*), crying out "Would to God I had never left!" (*The Father and Daughter*), or leaving pathetic notes: "This night I became wretched wanderer from thy paternal roof! Oh, that the grave were this night to be my lodging! . . . I think I could meet my heavenly father with more composure and confidence than my earthly parent!" (*The Coquette*). When Charlotte Temple's letters home go astray, her depressed state is such that she assumes her parents are either dead or have cast her off forever, and abandons hope of even their forgiveness. Similarly, when Adeline's letters to her mother are intercepted, she does not even suspect it.

Such fears seem all the more remarkable in view of the fact that the parents in question (excepting Adeline's) are not portrayed as bad ones: On the contrary they are careful, loving, and forgiving. But their daughters, like Emmeline when faced with good fortune, are persistently "doubtful of the evidence of [their] senses" and they act in terms of a fantasy of a punishing, rejecting parental object. They *must* be cast off, abandoned or hated, because they have ruptured that magic domestic circle that encloses only one conscious relationship, that of parent and child. The mechanism here, it is important to note, is hardly the one of oedipal rivalry and threat: These are not girls who willingly assume a role of mature sexuality! The threat to the domestic circle is the far more primitive one of simple separation. These young women, despite (or through) their various horrid pregnancies, are portrayed as *unable to survive sex*, unless the mother or a proper substitute has been making the proper social and legal arrangements for it, for them. Sex annihilates, for they are children still, with a child's need for the relief of punishment. Here we have the key, I believe, to the popularity of this repeated story of mutual·abandonment, of foolishness and flight and punishment. The family alone seemed a possible stabilizing force in the early national period; the invention of moral motherhood was to act as a further stabilizer. The family circle must not only be "sacred" in a new way; those who embodied that sacred quality must be prevented from losing it, by heavy sanctions against encountering the world's corruptions. What better sanction than the lifelong prohibition against adult status?

In a fantasy world where the only deeply felt human relationship is one of utter dependence, any threat to this relationship is particularly dangerous. That these girls are not punished by their parents, but by the social order enclosing the family circle, illustrates only how fictional fantasy is useful to, in fact supports, the ideology of its historical time and place. Throughout, we will see a change in the relationship, in how it is expressed, symbolized, and valued. Yet the fundamental nature of the dependency will not change.

In this group of novels, money is, after emotional rhetoric, the chief way in which dependency is expressed and symbolized. A young woman is owned (by father or husband), gambled for (the gay deceiver), or stolen (the abductor). This is traditional value. Economic difficulties account, as they do in the traditional realistic novel, for a number of twists and turns in plot: attempts to force a marriage, debts or poverty that prevent a marriage (this, in half our stories),[87] penury as punishment, or modest inheritance as happy ending. During the years in question, there are no exceptions to the rule that the heroine of a popular novel sold in America is unable to support herself. That this idea is no great distortion of social reality in either England or America is not a sufficient explanation for the way these books portray the attempt as a violation of womanly nature.

Only two of these heroines make any attempt to support themselves. Adeline, against masculine advice, tries to start a school, which she loses as soon as word of her "past" gets about.[88] But her first response to financial need was to write home to her mother for help. Laura, in *Self Control*, has plans to make a living with her painting, looking forward to "wealth and independence" with "ardour." She acquires neither. The man who will eventually become her husband subsidizes her, as the mysterious purchaser (at twice the asking price) of all her work, and long before the story's end she is living in other people's houses, under their protection, because it is not possible that she should live alone; she has also quit painting. In *Clarentine*, the heroine, "without any natural friends and assured support" has a fortune anonymously settled on her by *her* eventual husband.

Like Adeline, Charlotte Temple writes home for money when abandoned by her lover, but also to no avail, since the letters go astray. "How must [her] depression be encreased, when, upon examining her little stores, she found herself reduced to one solitary guinea, and . . . in debt." But she *does nothing.* "Never," comments the author, "did any human being wish for death with greater fervency or with juster cause," and the landlady who suggests that Charlotte perform manual labor for a wage is characterized as an "unfeeling wretch."

Economic independence would require that these women (as it legally required of the women who wrote and read these books) do without the protection of any male relative or guardian, let alone a husband,[89] and this is a possibility they dare not entertain. Indeed, if one of them discovers (like Emmeline, Constantia, or Louisa) that she is in fact no orphan but legitimate heiress to a fortune, her second act (the first is to express passionate gratitude for the fact that her parents loved her after all) is to turn it all over to that substitute for parents, her husband. In *Constantia*, this transaction is especially elaborate: Her lover, the son of the false marquis who usurped her father's place, must apply to her for the money in foreign banks which his father salted away under her father's name. "I bring with me . . . memorandums, that will enable my Constantia to make a poor man rich, if her heart remembers the affiance, which in his more prosperous days he sealed upon her hand!" Her heart remembers, as, indeed, women's "hearts" are expected to do throughout the Romantic and Victorian eras. The unconscious mechanisms that cause a very carefully reared girl to depend for her sense of self on her emotional relation to others fit very neatly with the ideology of developing industrial society. Women are to stay home and reproduce workers for that world: refreshed and gratified husbands, and sons for the Republic—both under a moral influence supposed to be good for business.

It is a commonplace of psychoanalytic thought that even the most bizarre behavior is an attempt to cope with the individual's reality. The collective reality that these fictions portray again and again includes a profound ambivalence about mothers and motherhood. Both can be terrifying, even lethal. On the other hand, mother is the great love of a woman's life, and motherhood (licit, *married* motherhood with its exclusive opportunities for justifying one's existence) can make life worth living. No service is too demanding to perform for a mother, or her substitute in father, husband, child. Abandoning mother, like abandoning one's child or husband is, for a woman, the unforgiveable sin, and can be atoned for only by death or by becoming utterly dependent on someone else.

This ideal view of woman's role in the unstable society of the new Republic hastened the transition to the Victorian style of middle-class mothering.[90] It is easy to imagine that the sons of the middle class in this period in America, reared to independence, to *citizenship*, were less oppressed by "tender maternal cares, vigilant attention and incessant anxiety" (*Clarentine*) than were their sisters. The evidence provided us by the plots and themes and characterization of this body of fiction (which has no counterpart at all in the male world) suggests that the daughters of the Republic were *not* benefitted by the new amount of attention that was paid to them. The books are also, I believe, evidence that the women who wrote and read them felt trapped by the prevailing stereotype and its expectations for a life of true womanhood. And they were just sufficiently aware of their anger at this to enjoy some fantasy murders, and indulge in some fantasy reaction-formations—mother and baby worship, dire retributions, and the like.

If a child learns, as soon as she *can* learn, that everything is demanded of her in a love relationship, and is later taught that no other sort of relationship is permitted her, she will as a matter of course turn away from social realities other than those of the family. How, then, can she resolve the ambiguities and relieve the anxieties of her condition? Only in a fantasy world, of the worst and the best that could happen to a young woman within the limitations imposed by her condition.

This chapter has examined popular fiction from the years during which America first began to think (and feel) about mothering in the modern way. The formula for such fiction, we have seen, regularly requires an absent mother and a treacherous lover, and—in the heroine—emotional extremes of self-loathing and blissful merging with others. I have suggested that the intense terror and grieving of these heroines reflects new intensities in the mothering of daughters. The imagery of the split self and other, of imprisonment, and of persecution and abandonment, is drawn from gothic fiction and presented in the sentimental style. It is nonetheless the imagery of an inner world in which the self and the other are not differentiated, in which reward and punishment are mysterious and excessive, and in which female autonomy of any sort has no place. In the chapters that follow we will not find that women's popular fiction illustrates a steady line of psychological development, but we will see heroines exhibiting a greater degree of differentiation, a better grasp on the realities of the outer world, and some new attempts at autonomy.

The Texts

Page numbers of important references to these texts, as they appear in sequence in this chapter, follow each bibliographical citation.

An American Lady. *The Hapless Orphan or Innocent Victim of Revenge.* Boston: Belknap and Hall, 1793. (vol. II, 21, 110–121, 121)

Brunton, Mary. *Self Control.* Edinburgh, 1820. (vol. I, 7–8, 3, 8; vol. II, 305, 171; vol. III, 64; vol. I, 43; vol. II, 177; vol. I, 168, 128)

Burney, Sarah Harriet. *Clarentine.* Philadelphia: Carey and Son, 1818. (vol. I, 4, 98, 38, 203; vol. II, 198; vol. I, 4)

Foster, Hannah Webster. *The Coquette; or, The History of Eliza Wharton.* Boston: E. Larkin, 1797. (228, 235, 231)

Helme, Elizabeth. *The History of Louisa, The Lovely Orphan; or, The Cottage on the Moor.* Boston: Samuel Etheridge for William Spotswood, 1798. (9th edition) (93, 72)

Lee, Harriet. *Constantia de Valmont.* Philadelphia: Matthew Carey, 1799. (31 32, 42, 46 ff., 60, 101)

Lennox, Charlotte. *The Female Quixote; or, the Adventures of Arabella.* Edited with an introduction by Margaret Dalziel, London, 1970. (5, 340, 261, 373)

Opie, Amelia. *Adeline Mowbray.* Philadelphia: James Crissy, 1843. (The first American edition of her work was published in Boston in 1825.) (111, 113, 120, 136–137, 154, 181, 136, 137, 225)

———. *The Father and Daughter.* London: Longman, Hurst, Rees, Orme, and Brown, 1819. (82, 99, 126, 90, 1)

Roche, Maria Regina. Translated from the German. *Eliza: or The Pattern of Women, A Moral Romance.* Lancaster, Pennsylvania, 1802. (53, 65, 178)

Rowson, Susanna. *Charlotte Temple: A Tale of Truth.* From *Three Early American Novels,* edited with an introduction by William S. Cable, Columbus, Ohio, 1970. (The first American edition of this novel was published in Philadelphia in 1794.) (42, 128–129, 119, 109, 111)

Seward, Anna. *Amelia, or, The Faithless Briton, an original American novel, founded upon recent facts, to which is added Amelia, or Malevolence Defeated . . .* Boston: William Spotswood and C. P. Wayne, 1798. (61, 51)

Smith, Charlotte. *Emmeline, The Orphan of the Castle*. Edited with an introduction by Anne Henry Ehrenpreis, London, 1971. (The first American edition was published in Philadelphia in 1802). (256, 158, 6, 362)

————. *Montalbert*. Philadelphia: Mathew Carey, 1975. (vol. I, 101; vol. II, 2; vol. I, 52, 64)

Tenney, Tabitha. *Female Quixotism, or the Extravagant Adventures of Dorcasina Sheldon*. Boston: J. P. Peaslee, 1829. (6)

Warren, Caroline Matilda. *The Gamesters; or Ruins of Innocence, an original novel founded in truth*. Boston, 1805. (153)

3

LOVING THE ROOF:
The Later 19th Century

I. The Period

The social paradox that we observed in the last chapter received its fullest expression in the period that followed. Dramatic material success increasingly supplanted a contented competency as the goal of earthly existence and as the insignia of those destined for heavenly reward. The unique rhetoric of the young democracy, as well as the claims of American Protestant religion, insisted that financial prosperity was within the scope of any wide-awake, willing, hard-working, thrifty man. Capitalism—in its most aggressive, competitive form—opened the West, industrialized and urbanized the East, and sealed off the middle-class home ever more securely from the rest of the social world. As their standard of living rose, its women became increasingly less autonomous, and the cultural value of their new, nonmaterialistic, noncompetitive role rose and crystallized. Lower-class women often simply shifted their work from home to factory. Those women whose husbands could support their families by their own unaided efforts, however, became simultaneously status symbols and moral luxuries for their husbands.[91] American optimism pervaded and welded the private and public spheres, and "improvement" meant the railroad and temperance, the efficiency of monopoly and the rise of popular education, the North's triumph in the Civil War, revivalism, Manifest Destiny, and home comforts and the refinement of manners.

Nevertheless, in practical everyday terms, the two spheres were increasingly distinct, and as women went West they took the eastern middle-class family pattern and its ideology with them, chiefly aided by a northeastern industry: publishing.[92] In her role as spiritual and moral adhesive for this exploding society, the mother of civilization was given directives, comfort, and support by other women through the medium of print. After 1830, with the commercialization of the press, the production of fiction by native American writers increased rapidly,[93] though British stories continued to be read. (Two British examples are included in this chapter: the novels by Mary Higham and Catherine G. Ward.) Yet American versions of British Romantic and Victorian stereotypes are deployed and displayed in a new way, chiefly because of differences in the social hierarchy here.[94] American women's books dominated the literary market from the 1840s through the 1880s, incalculable in their influence,[95] not only because the fiction itself was a powerful carrier of the ideology of domesticity, but because many of the women who wrote the stories also wrote stories for children, or manuals for child-rearing or for housekeeping in general.[96] The women who wrote the books had practical experience with which to back up theory; many of them, in fact, wrote to support themselves and their families,[97] although at first they were not eager to characterize themselves as competitors in the literary marketplace.[98] This, after all, would be a denial of the very views they were popularizing. A sense of a very real "calling" to writing as a vehicle for social redemption seems to have sustained them. Women speaking to women, they were enthusiastic about the special qualities they believed to belong to their sex, and earnest in a desire to cherish and develop and use these qualities.[99]

The prescribed socialization of boy and girl children continued to be quite different throughout this period.[100] Girlhood became an intensive training ground for the emotions appropriate to the domestic role: first, of course, the romantic love that alone legitimized wifely status, but also (of equal if not greater significance) maternal love, and spirituality. In the novels of the antebellum years, children's and women's fiction began to overlap, as heroines grew younger and younger in order that a longer and longer probation period might be undergone before they were fictionally elevated to the almost divine status of wife and mother.[101] Before the Civil War, images of childhood as a period of innocence co-exist with the frequent theme of the necessity to inculcate self-control in the child, especially in the little girl. (Boys are allowed a much greater degree of rebelliousness and even irresponsibility, provided of course that they repent and amend their behavior.) After the war, the child of either sex tends to become one of many symbols in the national litany of nostalgia for a purer age.

The antebellum domestic novel has been characterized by one scholar as depicting a heroine without external aids, making her success in life "entirely a function of her own efforts and character,"[102] her identity dependent on neither father nor husband. I think it can be shown that these fathers, indeed, are portrayed as having lost much positive influence on their daughters' lives.[103] Yet this formulation, while it marks an important difference between these stories and earlier genres, leaves open the question of how much a heroine's identity may be dependent on her mother's. Fairly often, the heroine begins to make her way in life in reaction against a father's tyranny (which is, however, effectual only where a mother is absent) or against a mother's foolishness, debility, and weakness—yet this will never prompt her to cut family ties completely if she can maintain them, repair broken ones, or, as a last resort, create new ones as much as possible like the old.

In sharp contrast to the heroine of the early national period, she is fairly certain of her value, and of what constitutes right and wrong behavior for her (though just how she knows this is often, in view of her innocence, quite mysterious). She is seldom a victim of novel-reading; she has, instead, the healthy habit of Bible-reading, and tries to obtain what education she can, as well. She is rarely (but not *never*)[104] in danger of seduction. One writer speaks of these books as simultaneously glorifying the common woman for her endurance and dependability and taking revenge on men for their frivolity and untrustworthiness.[105] The glorification in fact inheres in a special notion of dependability; unless one of these heroines has attained a condition in which someone else needs her desperately, her work is all in vain and her independence an empty shell. The untrustworthiness of men is shown just as clearly to be a pattern they are deliberately indulged in—unlike little girls— from early childhood, often by the heroines themselves. Nevertheless, not all the men in these fictions are spoiled by such indulgence, as we will see.

These heroines, unlike those of the earlier period, do not die if they depart from the family circle, because they simply never voluntarily depart from it; they take it with them. Furthermore, if they are orphaned, they create it anew for themselves. They do so in a variety of ways and guises, but some themes are very regularly repeated. We will examine these now.

II. Feminine Innocence: The Image of the Child

To explain this phenomenon, we must examine how the twin issues of innocence and experience are treated in this group of books. In the early national period, there were two ways of viewing a child: through the Calvinist concept of original sin, and through the Enlightenment idea of the *tabula rasa*, "to which Americans, following Scots, attached an embryonic moral sense."[106] At the end of this period, however, a new approach appeared, properly termed Romantic. It characterized the child as possessed of a positive, inborn goodness, which needed only to be developed to assure her of salvation.[107] This change in attitude was consistent with the period's greater interest in children. It was also most helpful as a support for the image of home as a refuge from worldly evil. To complete that image, only one detail needed to be added: that of a mother whose inborn goodness has encountered no tarnishing badness in the course of its development.

We are concerned here, therefore, not with the helpless, hopeless innocence of the heroines in the last chapter, whose repression of sexuality appears to have been entirely unconscious, managed by parents, hence equally manipulable by a rapacious male.[108] The heroines of this chapter *sublimate* their sexuality in work, religion, and especially, the maternal "instinct." But their sexual innocence is preserved by their own efforts; by their delicacy and deliberate caution. For, often enough, they have no protectors, or—as we will see—discover the most powerful threats or temptations where protection should be.

This makes the task of growing up to be a mature woman an arduous one, so that we should not be surprised to find that the journey is often not completed—even, at times, ends in a retreat. "I don't want to be a little woman. I never will be one," (*Rena; or, The Snow Bird*) says one child heroine after another, faced with the enormous task of reconciling the irreconcilable contradictions in the role expected of her. (Some even wish they were boys; for example, the heroine's rash foster sister in *Mary Derwent.*)

Hentz, in 1852, describes a female child: "A beautiful child is certainly the most beautiful object in the world. The incarnation of innocence, sweetness, and grace; fresh from the hands of its Creator, before temptation has obscured, or sin marred or passion darkened the image of the Deity; it comes before the world-weary eye, a flower sparkling with the dews of Paradise, and breathing the fragrance of Heaven" (*Rena*). In this unmistakably Romantic view, one expects to find a description of our child heroine—in fact, it is a description of the villainness of the story, Stella Lightner. The real heroine, Rena, is "a child of impulse, enthusiasm, sensibility . . . the wildest of the wild . . . . [Her mother] was a scrupulously neat lady. She never allowed a fold of her dress to be out of place, or a spot to sully its purity. Rena was the most careless little creature in the world. She was always tearing her frocks . . . ." Throughout the early portion of the novel, the two children are contrasted: The one, through vanity, becomes cold and deceitful; "the simplicity of childhood had no charm for her," while Rena "did not care how she looked; all she wanted was to be loved" saying "my own self [is that] for which only I would be loved."

The ambiguities here are not unusual, since in this whole group of stories a difference between the appearance and the reality of the female characters is of fundamental thematic importance. In Southworth's *Allworth Abbey*, for example, the heroine, on whose innocence of a crime the plot depends, is a dark Southern beauty, and much (in the English setting) is made of this "paradox." Rena, child of nature, has thereby access to a higher truth—but she must also (literally) learn to keep her hat on! Variants of this problem beset all the heroines in their struggle to retain the "simplicity of childhood," that is, to be faithful to their mothers. And in all the stories, moreover, the young women who are foil and often enemy to the heroine are characterized by their worldliness and ambition. The experience that destroys innocence is escaping the mother's domestic sphere of influence, not rivaling her. We will return to this topic.

Child heroines enliven the opening pages of Hentz's other novels, Holmes's *Lena Rivers*, McIntosh's *Emily Herbert*, Warner's *Wide Wide World*, and Terhune's *Alone*—to name but a few. Rena's mother is one of the many frivolous invalids who crowd the pages of these books; other girls are orphaned. Ida, of *Alone*, is orphaned in her 15th year "the age of all others when a mother's counsel is needed;—when the child stands tremblingly upon the threshold of girlhood . . . . Babes in knowledge, nine girls out of ten are grown in heart at fifteen." Ida's mother was a "scarcely less than divine" figure. (*Wide Wide World* contains an extended comparison of the mother's and the Savior's love.) How to imitate this? How to preserve, in Mother's absence, that unspotted self which was her gift to her daughter?

III. Feminine Innocence: The Mother's Image

The new sacred and delicate (or dead) mother of these stories cannot deserve too much careful handling. As MacLeod says of the mothers in the children's fiction of the 1850s, "Her children might be called upon to protect or comfort her, and this they were more than ready to do, for their attachment to her was in some tales emotional and sentimental in the extreme."[109] In Hentz's *Ernest Linwood*, for example, the child heroine prays, "I will drink the cup of poverty and humiliation to the dregs if thou wilt, without a murmur, but spare, O spare my mother!" Having, under the newly intensive moral guidance of the period,[110] internalized Mother's saintly model, a daughter's problem is "How can I be grateful enough to her?" (*Lucy Howard's Journal*) "I think I am in love with my beautiful mother," continues this particular child heroine. "She is so young for her years, so graceful in all her ways . . . . Our confidence is perfect. I tell her every plan and every thought . . . ." And, in adulthood, "This perfect confidence is precious. It seems always due to the being who has borne so much for us. I can scarcely imagine how it could be otherwise."

Over and over again, "perfect confidence" between mother and daughter is portrayed and praised—a symbiotic fusion of minds and emotions. "Because of their mothering by women, girls come to experience themselves as less separate than boys, as having more permeable ego boundaries," observes Chodorow, of the developmental pattern called "normal."[111] "Neither party to this close and inevitably ambivalent relationship can be ordinarily free and resilient in a relationship to the outer world, and the maintenance of this too tight little mother–child unit may have far-reaching and sometimes disastrous effects on the child's subsequent development," most especially where the child is a daughter.[112] The pre-oedipal attachment of daughter to mother can act to sustain "the mother–infant exclusivity and the intensity, ambivalence and boundary confusion of the child still preoccupied with issues of dependence and individuation."[113] It cannot be otherwise in a culture where mothering is described as "a mirror, in which thy smiles and tears shall be reflected back; a fair page, on which thou, God-commissioned, mayst write what thou wilt; a heart that will throb back to thine love for love . . . the maternal eye must never sleep at its post . . ." (*Ruth Hall*).

In the fiction of the early national period, the cast of characters seemed to be drawn from the fantasies which Klein and others attribute to the very earliest stages of psychological development: an inner world of all-good or all-bad beings. In such unconscious fantasies the other is divinely gratifying, or else totally malignant. The self is pure, or it is corrupted. Such images are comparable, as we have seen, to Jungian concepts of maternal archetypes, and of the parts of the individual psyche. In those stories of seduction, gothic horror, and abandonment, no healing of these splits in the self and with the other is portrayed. The sensations of terror and bliss predominate. The heroine either deserves to die or to be granted (she does not *earn*) the absolute security of perfect love. In this later group of stories there appears a constellation of emotions associated with a later developmental stage. These heroines of the domestic fiction of the mid-19th century work very hard indeed, in a variety of ways, to *earn* love.

The earlier fantasy world is not replaced entirely; it is only covered over. Yet here at this level the split between good and bad may be healed, and the other and self seen—at least temporarily—whole. According to psychoanalytic theory, at this later stage of development the child's leading anxiety is no longer fear of punishment, but of *destroying what she loves herself*. This anxiety is accompanied by a powerful desire for what Klein terms *reparation*. She described this capacity for love and concern as the *depressive position*, to clarify her point that it is not a stage one passes through and leaves forever behind.[114] The heroines of mid-19th century fiction fall into the depressive position with uncanny regularity—whenever, that is, they fall short of what they take to be their mother's demands on them.[115]

To pass beyond this phase of development and to move out of this ever-tightening circle, some aggression is necessary.[116] Yet what daughter *could* express aggression against these mothers, all either perfect saints (so that one's own frustrations and anxieties seem trivial), or perfected in heaven, or in need of maternal care themselves? For example, some of these mothers are "feeble-minded and self-indulgent" (*Ellen Parry*) and must be supported, literally, by their daughters, while others have been so victimized by bad men that their daughters must mother themselves. The heroines, in each case, can be seen as re-creating in themselves the fantasized and longed-for "good" mother, who is idealized *in proportion* as the "bad" mother is hated and feared for her abandonment of her child. The importance of this particular mechanism, in the symbolism, imagery, and resolutions of this group of stories can hardly be overemphasized.

In Terhune's *The Hidden Path*, the mother whom Bella "had reverenced as a being too pure and good to be the mate of any but an angel in heaven, had wedded a man she [Bella] could not love or respect, although forced to call him by that angel-father's name . . . . It was, in her eyes, a deliberate cold-blooded severing of the bonds, which nature and love had knit about them . . . . But she uttered not a syllable." Bella attends her mother's deathbed in an "agony of solicitude" about 375 pages later, still regarding her mother as "pure in heart," primarily because *she, Bella*, has kept her image of her mother pure! Victimized by a sadistic cynic, the heroine of *Alone* exclaims to him that "I have driven back the tears until the scalding waves have killed whatever in my soul could boast a heavenly birth. There is nothing there to prove my relationship to my mother, but her memory. When that is destroyed, I shall go mad." It is not destroyed, and because she is able to preserve it, Ida's destiny is a happy one.

In Ann Stephens's *Mary Derwent*, the heroine is a cripple because her mother, in a fit of (postpartum?) insanity, "in the wild fancy that [Mary was] an angel that could help her up to heaven . . . seized [her] in her arms, one day, and dropped [her] from the high window . . . ." Mary's predictable reaction, upon first hearing this tale, is "In a little time I shall see her . . . no one shall tend her but myself; I am her oldest child; never till now did I know what a mother was; how pleasant the sound . . . ." In this case the idealized fantasy image of mother has preserved itself over decades in the heroine; one of the determining dynamics in unresolved symbiosis between mothers and daughters who are not parted. In Amanda Douglas's *Home Nook*, Jessie cannot bear the thought of departing from her (impoverished) home and mother and sisters for marriage to her (wealthy) lover: "How could they do without her?"

In McIntosh's *Violet; or, the Cross and the Crown*, an even more complicated change is rung on the theme of taking care of mother; the heroine believes herself to be the true child of a rough sailor and his wife, though her "inborn delicacy" causes her to experience extraordinary agonies as she is properly submissive and dutiful toward this hard and vulgar pair. After she learns she is *not* their child, she still has difficulty in not calling the woman "mother"—her first thought on regaining consciousness after a narrow brush with death is to inquire after *her* welfare.

In Gilman's *Love's Progress*, a mysterious void separates the child heroine, Ruth, from her mother; "no trusting love nestles on her pillow." At the dangerous age of 15 she weeps "in secret with a bitterness that should only belong to sin and experience," and feels "often unloved and lonely." Religious experience comes to console her, and none too soon, for her mother, dying, elicits a promise from Ruth "I will be to my father as a child what you have been to him as a wife." In other words, a mother. He is, in fact, quite mad, but Ruth stays with him, despite her fiancé's commands. "Away, tempter!" she tells him, "The only asylum for my father is near his child's breaking heart." Finally her father tries to drown her and is drowned himself in the attempt, while her fiancé rescues her. His comment is "I know that the tender *daughter* will be the faithful *wife*."[117] A similar estimate of feminine character is made at one point in the British novel, *The Mysterious Marriage; or, The Will of my Father*: Rosa as a child would "eagerly fly to the maternal bosom and almost dissolve in kisses . . . this sensibility has continued . . . when she forms attachments they will be lasting." Indeed, each partner in a symbiotic relationship is threatened, as if by death, by any thought of separation. Another father, this one supposedly in prison, is a daughter's holy charge, for a mother's sake. "I remembered her dying injunctions," the heroine reports, "I thought of the heaven which he had forfeited . . . I wanted to go to him,—to minister to him in his lonely cell . . . to lead him to . . . the heaven from which my mother seemed stretching her spirit arms to woo him to her embrace." Gabriella's mother (*Ernest Linwood*) had dreamed that her daughter was "the guardian angel" of the father's soul, therefore her mission must be fulfilled. The maternal role, with its imperative of salvation for all men of the family, must never be rejected, no matter what it means for the daughter who assumes it in her mother's place.

This is the model of feminine behavior upon which these stories are based. The equation is nowhere obscured; in fact it is frequently made explicit. A good wife is, exactly and only, *both mother and child*, "so simple, so gentle, with all a child's purity and guilelessness, yet with a woman's sweet reserve," as the hero of *Violet* muses of the girl who "redeems" him. When she promises to marry him, she reminds him twice that she "will not cease to be [her true, found, father's] child in becoming [a] wife." She even insists on obtaining her foster mother's consent.

When Gabriella, in *Ernest Linwood*, admits to herself that she cannot "recall the guileless simplicity of childhood, its sweet unconsciousness and content, in the present joy" of her new love for Ernest, she has a vision of her departed mother that seems to "dim the bright image reflected in the mirror."

"O foolish, foolish Gabriella!" she mourns. "Art thou no longer a child?" Perhaps not. But she is certainly to be her husband's mother, for her good angel tells her that she "will be the forbearing, gentle wife, who promised to *endure all* . . . . You dare not murmur," and Ernest's real mother tells her "Be strong, be patient, be hopeful, and you shall yet reap your reward," when he is apparently unfaithful to her.

The transfer is seamless. There is always a mother, caring. A young woman may, in this body of fiction, attempt a period of independence, when not faced with the alternative of starvation, but it is not presented as a good thing for anyone. The young women suffer for it in a number of ways.

IV. Feminine Experience: Work Outside the Home

When she proposed to leave her home after her grandparents' death, Edna Earl of Evans's *St. Elmo* is asked, "But where could you go, and how could you make your bread, you poor little ailing thing?" She is subsequently prevented from working in the mills by an injury sustained in a train wreck, which results in her being adopted and educated by none other than the hero's mother. A similar intervention, or else sheer nervous exhaustion, over-whelms each young woman's effort at entry into the public sphere of work, no matter what her need or provocation. This sort of experience, *more than any*, is portrayed as destructive of woman's innocence. To see how strongly this is felt, we need only to examine some of the strong provocations to financial independence that are sustained by these heroines.

Hentz's Eoline's father attempts to force her into a loveless marriage. "It was solely to preserve from legal desecration, the as yet lonely but pure inner temple of her spirit that she was about to flee." When she becomes a teacher, it is, furthermore, explicitly and frequently stated that she is *not* doing it solely for her own spirit's purity, but also for the sake of her intended husband's happiness. Other young women with excuses for jeopardizing their innocence in jobs are Evans's Beulah and Terhune's Bella, as well as Holmes's Marian Grey and Southworth's Alice Chester in *The Discarded Daughter*, whose guardian and father, respectively, try to force them into loveless marriages. In fact, this sort of paternal behavior replaces the role of the seducer as the important image of persecution in this group of novels. This reflects, as we will see, a transformation of the images of men between this body of fiction and that described in Chapter Two.

Beulah is perhaps the most striking of all these heroines in her "proud nature," which makes the mere thought of dependence "galling to her." (Also she has had her emotional dependents taken from her by force: her sister adopted and her "friend" sent abroad.) When, at 12, she has been forced to leave the orphan asylum, she is removed from a dreadful position as child's nurse by the mysterious, aloof Dr. Hartwell. She determines to accept his support only until she can qualify as a teacher, refusing to be adopted and thus endangering the inheritance of his niece. Her friend, Clara, has this to say: "Beulah, you are mad to dream of leaving him and turning teacher . . . . Be warned, Beulah; don't suffer your haughty spirit to make you reject the offered home that may be yours . . . . Oh, Duty is an icy shadow! It will freeze you. It cannot fill the heart's sanctuary. Woman was intended as a pet plant, to be guarded and cherished; isolated and uncared for, she droops, languishes, and dies." Beulah contemptuously rejects the image of a "sickly geranium" for herself and says that for her, Duty is "a vast volcanic energy." Later we find her living "in a perpetual brain fever, and her physical frame suffering proportionably." "Oh child! are you trying to destroy yourself?" Dr. Hartwell asks rhetorically, and she admits she is daily growing weaker, trembles when she stands and walks, and can't sleep. But she will not rest; she sends him away and continues to write an article to prove that woman's happiness is not necessarily dependent on marriage, though "weary work it all seemed to her now."[118] She cannot marry him as he now desires, because she has loved him "as a child adores its father"—just as she had to leave his house, refusing adoption, because she loved him not exactly as a child!—and it takes three more years and her return to the Bible and prayer before she recognizes the void in her heart.

Terhune's Bella, unlike Beulah, returns a man's love early in her independent career, and will not marry him to become "a clog upon every step of [his] career . . . a fatal blow to his advancement . . . ." She declares to her wicked stepfather that she will "not be dependent upon anyone." Her "obstinate reserve prevent[s] her taking advantage of her mother's susceptible, affectionate disposition" and unveiling the stepfather's deception of them both. At the school where she goes to teach, she meets a spinster teacher who remarks of her career, "For forty years I have been *homesick*" [italics mine] and Bella herself loathes the work: "Lord: how long?" she cries, and "No captive Israelite ever raised the lamentation with more fervor." Yet she works on until the "action of her mind [is] retarded, if not weakened, by two years of drudgery . . ." and she needs a whole year as a house guest to recover her health. Similarly, Caroline Chesebro's Amy Carr falls prey to a "nervous fever brought on . . . by overwork and anxiety" while Edna in *St. Elmo* suffers "hypertrophy of the heart,"—no metaphor, she has painful attacks—because of her incessant mental labor. Subsequently she is accused (having written a popular book) of having "abused her constitution," and she is ordered to "read nothing, write nothing" while on a European jaunt—on pain of early death.[119]

In Chapter Two we saw debility, both physical and mental, become an important element in the plots of stories at the point where the heroine had committed a serious *sexual* transgression beyond the bounds of the family. Here, heroines do not so transgress; they are too delicate and careful for *that*. Yet the plots of these stories mete out nearly the same severe punishment for transgression against another canon of ideal womanly behavior, that a woman's work is in the home: She is too weak for the "world."[120]

This notion bears very little resemblance to the reality of the situations of all but the most wealthy women in the United States during these years. Housework was, for most of them, continuous, exhausting drudgery which they escaped only by becoming ill.[121] It is clearly a fantasy we have to deal with here, the fantasy that a young woman will be contaminated, soiled, and will lose her purity, if she enters the male sphere of work rather than remaining, supported by a man, in "her own." I do not mean to suggest that this fear had no basis in fact. It did. But in these story plots, the realistic depiction of loss of sexual innocence is regularly prevented by an illness that puts the heroine *safely to bed at home*, frequently for months.

In *Ernest Linwood*, Gabriella agrees to an early marriage, escaping from "experience," because her lover cries out "wait till she loses the freshness and simplicity that won me . . . . Wait till she has been flattered and spoiled by a vain and deceiving world . . . . No! give her to me now . . . in the bloom of her innocence, the flower of her youth, and I will enshrine her in my heart as in a crystal vase . . . ." Lucy Howard, as a mother, discovers "a new beauty in the name of *husband* since it is associated with that of *father* . . . . Around them cluster all those images of protection, reliance, and love, which our weaker sex needs from the loftier." The warning is clear: A woman's purity is safe only in the sheltered repetition of the ideal mother's role. None of these heroines, however orphaned, betrayed, or neglected by mothers, is without her fantasy of what a "good" one is like, and each is able to match the image perfectly at story's end. Even Edna endures this recital by her husband: "Accomplish thou my manhood, and thyself,/Lay thy sweet hands in mine and trust to me"; while Ida, as a wife, appears "younger, in face and manner, at twenty-seven than she was at [ambitious] seventeen . . . . Submission is a pleasure, not a cross."

The concept of feminine innocence is inseparable from that of a childlike reverence for a parent figure. Woman's moral influence depends on her purity, and can only be exerted through love relationships that are explicitly *not* maturely sexual, but some variant on the mother–child relationship. "Passionlessness" in women, moreover, gave them another real, if small, influence over the family by helping them to limit it in size.[122] Yet this may well have aided in the narrowing of focus and energy in both male and female spheres. A mother could concentrate her attention more intensely on the few children she now had at home, while male energies could be sublimated in a greater investment in the workplace.[123] Finally, mother's sexual "delicacy" was a real fact as well as a fantasy. Maternal mortality was high, as were the rates of lingering complications: an important impetus to the concept of the delicate mother.[124]

V. Feminine Experience: The Loveless Marriage

There is, however, another sort of "experience" that destroys the innocence of young women in these stories. A loveless marriage is not only "revolting, disgusting, horrible!" (*The Discarded Daughter*); it, like a man's job, usually produces the symptoms of insanity that, in the fiction of the early national period, were reserved for the young woman who had been seduced and abandoned. In this group of texts, live fathers who are neither sadistic brutes, nor weaklings tied to a fashionable or whining wife's apron strings, are rarely portrayed. It perhaps goes without saying that guardians and fathers-in-law tend to be worse. In any case, a woman may go to a love match in a "childlike, submissive spirit" (Bessie in *Anna Clayton*). She may even have these qualities developed and/or rejuvenated by her marriage. But a loveless marriage is another matter. Anna Clayton's father makes her marry a man who subsequently goes to England, taking their two children with him. Anna's father sees the error of his ways: "Would to God . . . that reason may never return to mock, with its terrible truth, my heart-broken child!"

In Sedgwick's *Hope Leslie*, Alice loses her true love, and in "the imbecility of despair" marries another, so she "suffer[s] a total alienation of mind" and must live in absolute retirement. Alice in *The Discarded Daughter* feels that during her bridal tour "she had . . . lost her identity, seeming to herself to be someone else," and everything appears to her as "phantasmagoria . . . grotesque or hideous visions"; the return home is initially even worse. In *Eoline*, the heroine escapes her father's power, and he, Glenmore, undergoes a change of heart when he meets a friend's child, Amelia, who sits "like a statue of stone, her large black eyes riveted on the floor, with an expression of hopeless despondency." "If you love your daughter," this young woman's father tells Glenmore, "never let her marry a man whom she does not love with all her heart and soul. Make her take the responsibility of her life's future out of your keeping." Eoline, however, will give it directly into the keeping of another.

Here is how Eoline describes what her lover must be to her: "He must be a pillar of strength on which I can lean and cling round in the storms of life . . . . Then the love he bears me must be illimitable as the Heaven, and boundless as the air. It must be firm as the mountains, and unfathomable as the ocean . . . . And last of all, he must love me . . . just because I am Eoline." It is fairly clear what sort of emotional attachment is being described here; it is that which a mother is supposed to feel for her child. No young man in any single one of these stories loves like this, though virtually all the young women share Eoline's expectations. When Ernest Linwood is jealous, Gabriella says "There is no evil I could not bear while we loved one another . . . . There is no sacrifice I would not make to prove my faith. Do you demand my right hand?—cut it off; my right eye—pluck it out;—I withhold nothing. I would even lay my heart bleeding at your feet in attestation of my truth." Indeed *her* love for *him* replicates the ideal maternal model, but it is also clear that her reaction to his "returning love" is that of the forgiven child blissfully at one with the mother. "Oh, Audley," exclaims the heroine of *Little Sunshine*, "there are times when I wonder how you, so gifted and talented, can care for a childish and ignorant little creature like myself."

In *Lena Rivers*, there are two examples of loveless marriage; one brings death to the woman, the other merely creates one of "that most wretched of all beings, an unloving and unloved wife." In this novel, the matches are made by a villainous mother, for money, the motive that usually actuates parents in these cases. (Sometimes, as in *Violet*, the idea is to keep the inheritance in the family. For reasons that will become obvious, I will be discussing the proposed marriage in *Violet* in another context.) In *Mary Derwent*, the heroine's mother must sacrifice her true love. In her grief and madness she forgets her pain at losing him, and turns again "to the soft fancies and pleasant feelings of childhood," or will "weep and sing with a child-like sorrow." Precisely. The love relationship that is entered into by all these heroines is the love for a mother substitute, which, being denied, turns into abandonment depression.[125] The sense of self of these heroines is portrayed as dependent on their relationship with others; they lose it, if such a relationship is ruptured or cannot be achieved. Really to be alone, Winnicott says, requires the existence in the individual's psychic reality of a good sense of the other, available for projection.[126] Yet if this image *is* projected, and then *taken away*, in the person of the true-love, or even a young mother's children, the psychic emptiness that results is intolerable.

Such projections and losses occur often in these stories. In *Nameless* we meet a heroine who moves very rapidly to fill her emptiness. In public, Lady Haughton exhibits "no more trace of inward emotion than does a magnificent mountain on whose bosom sleep eternal snows," although in private she weeps passionate tears over a clandestine letter, which she burns with "a face as wan and painstricken as if she had burned away some integral part of herself." She has married Lord Haughton so that the letter-writer would not sacrifice a brilliant future for her, but after learning he is unworthy anyway, she reports that "a struggle began in my mind between the feeling evoked by the memory of the idol which my girlish imagination had created and the real living representative of goodness," her husband. Does she learn to feel a mature love for him, then? When she is through confessing all to her husband, she is "another woman . . . . Nestling . . . confiding . . . shy . . . kneeling at his feet."

VI. The Shadows of the Heroine

The men depicted in these texts, as I have suggested, are often drawn as unreliable. The rule is that they are to be trusted only after a rigorous period of probation; the pure love that sanctifies union is admitted only with great caution. No leap of the imagination is required to see in the defensiveness of these young women, whether expressed in pride, or modesty, or even humility, a *fear* of dependency equal to their need for it, and equal to their fear of mature sexuality. Unregenerate emotional and/or financial independence, and sexuality, then, are the property of female characters who are *not* heroines. In fact, only one other quality characterizes them, and it too is predictable, given the simplicity of the heroines: They are fashionable, greedy, snobs.

One of Caroline Hentz's shadow figures is Stella Lightner. Motherless and beautiful, she is resentful rather than grateful for charity, and deeply envious of the story's heroine, Rena. She is also a thief and goes to work as a milliner in the city. "You have taken a very extraordinary step, young lady . . . . It was rash and unadvised." (Rena *never* does such a thing!) Stella's greediness is early prefigured in the story when she steals apples; her punishment is an early death from consumption, though she is granted religion before her death. Another of Hentz's shadow figures (a type recurring throughout her work) is the "masculine" woman. In *Rena*, Aunt Debby is one of the "females with whom we ever can associate the idea of love,—who have such perfect unity of character, we never can imagine them as forming the *half* of another." We are to learn that this is the result of an early betrayal: "He has changed me into a being I myself abhor," Debby tells Rena, and subsequently she softens into a womanly woman under the child's influence. This redemption of the shadow figure is a new theme in this group of texts, illustrating in yet another way an attempt at real resolution of psychic splits.

In *Ernest Linwood*, another young woman is "feminized" by the heroine, although the schoolmistress, Miss Manly, in *Eoline*, remains impervious. "I have chosen my vocation, and never shall abandon it . . . . Let others seek happiness in the exercise of domestic virtues."[127] The cold and destructive condition Jungians call animus possession is not a characteristic of the women in these stories who seem like men, but rather of those heroines who deny their obligation of feeling.[128] The living death that overtakes the young women who try to be independent (Evans's heroines, Isabel, Ida) is the result of "that demon" getting fatter while the victim gets thinner, to use Von Franz's description. "She *has* to argue on," says Von Franz. The only thing to do is interrupt her; a piece of clinical advice these story's heroes do not need![129] The sexual ideology of midcentury is nowhere more clearly portrayed than in this seeming total inability to envision a character who has integrated the virtues assigned to the opposite sex.

Like Stella in *Rena*, Maria in Chesebro's *Amy Carr* leaves home, has her values corrupted, and steals money—this time the heroine's savings. She is saved by the forgiveness and example of the heroine. A secular salvation takes place also in McIntosh's *Emily Herbert*; here the child heroine forgives a rich and exceedingly unpleasant girl who mocks Emily's (new) poverty. When the wheel of fortune reverses their positions, Emily finds her, clothes her properly, and sends her to school.

In *The Discarded Daughter*, an inheritance prompts a young woman to an unbecoming independence: She does not accept a suitor's proposal of marriage. He exclaims in horror: "you will not become that monster of nature, a masculine woman—a—." She denies this somewhat obscure charge, only to hear from him that despite the fact that she is "ambitious, arrogant, scornful," she *must* marry him since they've toured Europe together (although chaperoned). This argument does not move her. "BEGONE. she thundered." Her mood changes, however, when *she* loves: "I thought to have conferred wealth upon you! It was a proud, presuming thought," she tells her husband-to-be. She renounces her estate at his request. "My wife!" he responds, and this shadow figure, at least, is redeemed.

Another shadow figure of considerable dramatic power is Tahmeroo, in *Mary Derwent*. She is the younger daughter of the Catharine who dropped her older ("angel") daughter from the window. Tahmeroo is no angel: Her father is the Indian chief Catharine now lives with in the American forest. In Tahmeroo, "the spirited and wild grace of the savage was blended with a delicacy of feature and nameless elegance more peculiar to the whites . . . full of warm healthy life . . . [and] fiery impatience." She acts out the abandonment and betrayal of her mother that a "good" heroine cannot. When Catharine discovers that Tahmeroo has a lover, his gift seems to her a serpent coiled around her daughter's hand, and when the sleeping girl whispers the man's name, Catharine snatches out a knife. "A moment the blade quivered above the heart of her only [sic] child . . . ." She reflects that "her absolute rule over that one soul had been to her a sovereignty, dear alike to her pride and to her affections. It had kept one well-spring pure in the depths of a wicked heart . . . her power over that heart must hereafter be one of love unmixed with fear—an imperfect and divided power." We need not look for a clearer statement of the nature of the mother–daughter relationship called unresolved symbiosis. Catharine's discovery that her older daughter still lives, together with Tahmeroo's running away to marry her lover, resolves the emotional issue for *her*: "Tahmeroo was henceforth her friend, her younger sister, but never again her child. To her, the thought was sacrilege." All emotional investment is withdrawn from the illegitimate savage, and transferred to the angel Mary. Upon Catharine's death, Tahmeroo becomes the chieftainess of her tribe; Mary assumes her English title while remaining "simple and childlike."

In *Lena Rivers*, similarly, the heroine's generosity and simplicity are contrasted throughout with the worldly selfish nature of the mother who pushes her daughters into the role of "unloving and unloved wife." In Evans's *Beulah* the most interesting of the female characters besides Beulah is the "joyless, cynical"—and rich—invalid, Cornelia Graham, with her "coterie of fashionable friends," whom she disdains: "Oh, Beulah, Beulah! child of poverty! would I could change places with you!" She illustrates, however, not only the proposition that wealth is destructive of feminine character; she is also badly damaged by the religious skepticism that *nearly* destroys Beulah. (For example, their despairing animus possession is illustrated in a long conversation about Emerson.) A similar character is that of Isabel, in *The Hidden Path*. Though she claims "I am a woman, weak and dependent, and not ashamed to avow it. I would not be what some miserable misguided fanatics call 'superior to my sex,'" she is still told quite firmly that her "robe of light" (she has published!) will turn to a "poisoned mantle, she would, but cannot tear away!" Her fame widespread, she becomes weary at heart, and mourns that she has separated herself from the "delicate and good" of her sex, illustrated, of course, in the heroine, Bella.

The symbolic device of poison figures in another way in *Allworth Abbey*. The heroine, suspected of being a prisoner, is unable to help herself. However, she meets a girl who says, "Oh, how I wish I were a boy! . . . I would like to go where I please, to do as I wish . . ." "What a misfortin [sic] it is for young creatures to lose their mothers!" thinks their landlady. "The one downstairs is a-going melancholy mad, and the one up here is gone merry mad." Annela's manic project is to save the depressed Eudora from hanging, which she appears to do by burning down the prison. Her "frenzy" then modulates into a long illness, after which the reader learns she did not really do it. The hero, who has also been helping, feels "infinite relief," and Annela's redemption from the shadow is confirmed by marriage to an officer of the Royal Navy.

There are other shadow figures in *Allworth Abbey*. The actual murderess, motivated by her "wrong," has kept her illegitimate daughter by her, in a relationship like that between Catharine and Tahmeroo. The girl has "never married; she was destined to another doom; to work her mother's will; to avenge her mother's wrongs. For this I kept her always near me; won her whole heart; absorbed her will; mastered her spirit . . . she had but one human affection—filial love." Not content with the double murder of one married couple, the mother who styles herself "THE AVENGER" has also disrupted another marriage by telling the pair they are half-brother and sister. This poisonous story causes another mother to wish her child (born, supposedly, of incest) dead, to isolate her from society, including her own, and to refuse to touch her. When she finally explains why, she warns that the knowledge "may kill you at once—strike you down dead before me! Be it so; better, you should die than live to marry." The Avenger's daughter suicides with poison, and the heroine is left with "deep wounds . . . [which] may possibly never be effaced in this world." Woman, the prisoner and devourer of children, surfaces in this particular book in a more than usually graphic fashion, but the core of terror and longing exposed is at the center of them all.

Certainly the figures of absolute evil are less interesting, just as they are less usual, than the shadows who are purged of their badness by the story's end. Characters in later, postbellum books by Southworth, Terhune, or Cummins first exemplify—only to ultimately disavow—worldliness, ambition, or independence. Even these texts do not, however, earn definition as novels,[130] since the transmutation into pure womanliness is so inflexible a convention. The culture's dreams fill the books' last pages, never the disillusion or unmasking of the novel. (The unmasking of pure badness is of course even more a device of the romance.)

VII. Becoming Mother

What quality, other than careful innocence, characterizes the "goodness" that these writers and readers dreamed of for women? Baym describes a plot formula that appears complete in six of the texts treated in this chapter, and in modified form in several others ". . . the heroine is a pampered heiress who becomes poor and friendless in mid-adolescence, through the death or financial failure of her legal protectors . . . at the end of the novel she is no longer an underdog. The purpose of [the plot] is to deprive the heroine of all external aids and to make her success in life entirely a function of her own efforts and character."[131] As I have suggested, the use of an orphan heroine hardly indicates the absence of maternal influence. Indeed, the influence of this group of fictional mothers appears to become even greater when it comes from beyond the grave. What is new, as a fantasy for getting rid of the mother who "rules the soul, absorbs the will, controls the destiny," is the reversal of mother/daughter roles, so that a daughter becomes Mother, herself. Lucy Howard, who despite her poetic genius leaves school gladly at 14, writes, "Now I can have time to help my darling mother. There is the strong consolation . . . if I can come with my young arm to the aid of that which so tenderly embraced me when a helpless infant . . . I shall be grateful and grieve no more." Emily Herbert accepts poverty: "Whatever else I may want, I certainly have the dearest mother in the world." "We are all the world to each other," claims another Lucy of her relationship with her widowed invalid mother in *Nameless*. Precisely. The strongest emotional imperative implanted in these heroines is to take care of someone, *to take Mother's place*.

Often this role is imposed as a matter of realistic necessity. When a heroine has a helpless mother and younger siblings, or her own children to support, she must also be frugal and work hard. Such conditions, by no means unfamiliar to the writers and readers of these books in real life, are portrayed by Lee's *Elinor Fulton*, Briggs's *Ellen Parry*, Parton's *Ruth Hall*, Terhune's *Hidden Path*, Child's *Romance of the Republic*, and Douglas's *Home Nook*. In *Elinor Fulton*, for example, the daughter must minister to her mother's "mind diseased," crippled, in fact, by a depression she calls ennui, since they have fallen in the world. Luckily Elinor knows that "There is no honest, industrious resolute individual but can find no means" to support herself and her family. Elinor teaches piano, and puts money by to help pay off her father's debts. "Blessings on the Savings Bank!" Yet when father comes home from the West, he characterizes marriage: "While he is laboring for the temporal benefit of the family, she may watch over its spiritual welfare . . ." and encourages Elinor to marry a successful architect so she can *do the same*.

The daughter who temporarily or permanently mothers her mother is common in this group of texts, and usually the mother is an inadequate or even "bad" one, so that the heroine can be seen to be re-creating in herself the fantasized and longed-for "good" mother which completes the romance's cast of characters. In *Ellen Parry*, Ellen's mother's training of her daughter has been "capricious and often unwise." Ellen rises above this to meet the test of insolvency. "My poor mother!" is her first thought, and she felt "that for her feeble-minded and self-indulgent mother, now too far advanced in life to make it probable that . . . adversity could bring her to conform with dignity to poverty—it was indeed terrible, awful." Ellen nurses her tenderly in her decline, refusing charity and conforming with dignity to poverty by becoming a teacher.

In *The Hidden Path*, Bella cannot let her mother be "mixed up in such a business" as her stepfather's double-dealing with her own inheritance. She conceals all from her mother, who dies of consumption, nursed by her daughter, with all her "innocence and ignorance" preserved.

An even more dramatic assumption of the burden in question appears in *Violet*. Violet goes to an extreme of stoic self-sacrifice in her nursing tasks. Though the woman is not her real mother, she does not yet know this; she only senses it. In reparation, then, for a mysterious lack of filial devotion, she has assumed the "Cross" of loyalty at her confirmation. She bears it with considerable difficulty: "Poor heart," we find her telling herself, "after all . . . it is not long; in a few years, perhaps in a few months, or weeks, or days . . . I shall go to my eternal home." Even after all is revealed (including her foster father's villainy) she calls the woman mother, and tries to care for her. Moreover, Violet's heart aches at the thought of leaving her *true* mother's remains alone when she departs with her husband and true father for England; she is only comforted when her father agrees to bring them along for reburial close to home.

Two heroines in this group of novels prove their inability to assume the nurturing role along with that of provider, by caring for their own children. In Child's *Romance of the Republic*, Rosa's first experience as a mother is doomed by her mental anguish over her husband's falseness and duplicity. She can't breastfeed her son: "Nature [is] deranged by bodily illness and mental trouble." She flees to Italy, becomes an opera singer, *marries* (though without giving up her very successful career) and successfully raises a daughter! In *Ruth Hall*, also, the heroine is an orphan at marriage. (Her father is alive, but cruel.) Her husband then dies, leaving her at the mercy of her sadistic in-laws. Two of her three children die, and her in-laws kidnap the other one. She goes to work for a newspaper—"She had not the slightest idea, till long after, what an incredible amount of labor she accomplished, or how her *mother's heart* was goading her on"—and gets her daughter back. The circle of family completes itself for her in a dream of all three children together again.

The selfishness, greed, passion, and envy of the shadow figures in these stories is contrasted, then, with the self-denial and self-control of the heroines. The two emotional configurations inevitably appear together. "When a person, whose sense of security is largely based on his greed," writes Riviere of the infantile personality, "sees that someone else has more than he, it upsets this self-protective edifice of security; he feels reduced to poverty . . . as if the others who have more must have actually *robbed* him . . . ."[132] Similarly, the sense of *having* enough corresponds in fantasy to *being good* enough. The America in which this group of stories was written and read provided a social context that aroused and prompted such primitive levels of response. The American national dream amplified, especially before the disillusionments of the Civil War, this same infantile fantasy of a split between the good as the comfortably well-off and the bad as the poor. "In the laboring class," Brown quotes Sedgwick as saying, "property is a sign of good morals . . . In this country nobody sinks into deep poverty, except by some vice, directly or indirectly."[133] Greed received, in effect, a religious sanction from those who preached material rewards in the here and now for anyone who would work for them. The personality type that saves both earthly gold and attempts to save souls for heaven came into its own. In fact, it was the national persona of that era, in Jung's sense of the term: a segment of the collective psyche.[134]

This amplification of a set of attitudes that helped to pile up wealth and property did nothing (during those years) to loosen the bonds of the family, where women and children could be regarded as property. Such regard was fostered by the "exclusive and intensive mothering" of the period, with its consequent "monogamic tendency." For young men, this was a convenient accompaniment to the high achievement orientation which appears also to follow on such childhood experience.[135]

Young women were already hampered in their desire for individuation by a relative inability to differentiate from the person upon whom they were earliest and most deeply dependent. For them, the cultural ban on achievement exacerbated the tendency to want one life-long exclusive relationship. What was a woman to do with *her* intensely self-disciplined and repressed personality? Besides saving souls, she was to *serve*! And of course she was to restore to mother all that had been taken from her in one's guilty desire to be different, by being as like her as possible instead. Supposedly separated from the mid-century's obsessive concern with *material* gain, women were nevertheless expected to perform prodigious tasks of service, physical, emotional, and spiritual. Laziness, in fact (always introduced in the texts in question as the result of being badly spoiled and indulged by a spoiled and indulged mamma) is as likely to define a "bad" woman in these fictions as greediness itself. "Good" women deny absolutely their need for the earthly reward of leisure but they get it all the same, as wives, at story's end. "You must promise to tell me every wish of your heart," Gabriella's husband informs her, "and be assured, if consistent with reason, it shall be gratified." This particular "good girl" is one of the most long-suffering wives to be met with in this body of fiction. What does she suffer from? Her husband's pathological possessiveness!

VIII. Home as Heaven

The rational bliss Ernest promises Gabriella is promised everywhere in these stories, as the very ambience of home. The line between home as locus of heavenly bliss and heaven itself, in fact, is often drawn very thinly. Sedgwick says: "A household, governed in obedience to the Christian social law [and implemented by] an uncompromising father and all-hoping mother, would present as perfect an image of heaven, as the infirmity of human nature . . . would admit" (*Home*), while Sigourney has her heroine state that she believes "home-happiness to be the secret of national prosperity," the means of social salvation, no less. "A home!" Isabel's husband reads aloud from his own essay on the subject. "The Lares of your worship are all there; the altar of your confidence there; the end of your worldly faith is there; and adorning it all, and sending you blood in passionate flow—is the ecstasy of the conviction that *there* at least you are beloved; that there you are understood; that there your errors will ever meet with gentlest forgiveness; that there your troubles will be smiled away; that there you may unburden your soul . . . be entirely and joyfully yourself!" The "infirmities of human nature" seem to have been temporarily forgotten; the love which is described as the "PRESENCE" of home is (like the mother love described in *Wide Wide World*) Christlike or better—it is the fusion of need with satisfaction, giving perfectly and unstintingly the oceanic bliss that Jungians identify as provided first by the "gods of our infancy."[136]

The women who are to dispense this supernatural bliss can experience it themselves only if they can transfer the emotional conditions of their girlhood homes to their married ones. And how they work to do so! Housework is the religious discipline of their days, and not only in the sense indicated by MacLeod's comment that there were "no limits to the demands of filial affection."[137] Girls were expected to be helpful before marriage in any household of which they were a part. Lena proves her worth in the home of the lazy and selfish Livingstones by cooking dinner when the servants are ill. Ellen, in *Wide Wide World*, has the whole care of the household on her shoulders when her aunt is ill, and it is very good for her: "Often in the midst of her work, stopping short with a sort of pang of sorrow and weariness, and the difficulty of doing right, she would press her hands together and say to herself, 'I will try to be a good pilgrim!'" It is not enough to pray oneself into patience, one must also be cheerful about the sacrifices and toil and, ideally, sing "like a bird that cannot restrain [her] song!" (*Lucy Howard's Journal*) while housekeeping. Violet advises her friend Louisa that her life's noble work can be to make her home "always orderly and pleasant" though she admits that "the most difficult thing in the world is, to bring ourselves to do common things cheerfully." Nothing less than such difficulty surmounted can replicate the full saintliness of the mother whom all these daughters agonize over leaving.

So hallowed is a particular home by the presence of a loving mother that an orphaned young woman can maintain that "The thought of being dragged from my home—from the sweet haunts which contained the precious remembrances of my parents—and conveyed to the cold, lordly halls of my aristocratic uncle, nearly flung me back to a state of delirium," (*Mary Derwent*) and in fact marry in order to go on living there. When Louisa, in *Eoline*, is orphaned, her friend Charles promptly asks her to "lighten the burden and temper the heat of his day of care" in *their* own home, and Eoline calls this opportunity to create a "firmament of peace and love . . . the greatest reward earth can bestow."

Anna, in *Lena Rivers*, is saved from madness by an elopement with Malcolm that forestalls the loveless marriage her unnatural mother wishes to force on her. Her mother repents, and yet when she begs her daughter to return home, Anna writes, "Tell mother I cannot come." This line ends the chapter, and its dramatic power depends on the fact that such a decision is unparalleled in this group of texts. Much more typical is Lucy Howard's reaction upon moving West with her husband. Of the separation from her mother, she writes, "Let me not think again of the parting embrace. *No, never,*" and when her mother joins them, "We shall be sundered no more. Have I ever before written words so full of joy?" In *The Mysterious Marriage,* the "gentle bosom of Rebecca could scarce sustain a parting with her mother, from whose tender care she had never been separated since the hour of her birth." In fact, these partings at marriage are depicted as no less painful and desolating than the deaths of mothers. The home of girlhood and its "PRESENCE" are sacred indeed; this is why the young married heroine will work so hard to restore it, in her own.

These stories show equally dramatic attachments of mothers to their children. When Ellen of *Wide Wide World* is parting from her dying mother, Mrs. Montgomery tastes "the whole of bitterness death ha[s] for her. . . . Death had no more power to give her pain after this parting should be over . . . it almost seemed to her that soul and body must part company too when they should be rent asunder." While girl heroines are shown as receiving a unique and indispensable form of emotional sustenance from their mothers, mothers, especially those who are widowed or abandoned, cling with similar desperation to their children as a source of emotional gratification. For example, when, in *Myra,* the heroine's betrayed mother has her child taken from her "she felt with keen intuition, which is like a prophecy, that she was not parting from her child for a season, but forever," and reacts with "utter insensibility," becoming "pale and deathly." Here it is the mother repeating the cry we have heard from bereft daughters, in *Alone, Wide Wide World, Ernest Linwood,* and elsewhere: "Alone—utterly alone! her child slept in the bosom of another!" and she dreams of the disappearance of her child and the father "leaving her prostrate and almost dead, to battle her way through the storm alone—alone!" The reader is reminded of Ruth Hall's dream of *her* lost children, when she is living alone, attempting to support the one left to her. Yet another maternal dream, described in *Anna Clayton,* illustrates the theme of the terror of separation: Anna has lost her children by a first, disastrous marriage. She has remarried, though "even in this hour of sacred joy, *the mother could not forget!*" Subsequently she falls fatally ill, and dreams of her death, but that an "angel of mercy . . . averts the dreaded shaft, and turning its face to her, murmurs 'Mother and home!' She sees her own image reflected . . . cries, 'My daughter—my own!'" The children actually do show up, and "the ebbing tide of life flows back into the mother's breast."

This life-or-death quality of the relationship is sometimes portrayed as extending beyond the grave; for Marcia, at the end of *Nameless*, feels "a mysterious and undissoluble blending of [her life] on earth with [that of her] angel [child]." Here again we see the association of a state of heavenly bliss with the mother–child relationship, rather than any other. This bliss belongs to the stage of "one common boundary" of mother/infant as an "omnipotent system"[138] of mutual gratification. Preserving the permeable ego boundaries of this stage fits girls for the affective role, of course, but it is shown as doing much more, in this body of fiction, so largely "about" self-definition. Symbiotically tied mothers and daughters may both be convinced that any separation between them will bring disaster to both. We have seen this conviction abundantly illustrated. The emotional significance of such terrors is also expressed in a number of fictional devices recurring throughout these texts.

IX. Themes of Salvation: Resurrection and Reincarnation

Besides the partings and the deathbed scenes, these writers and readers were extremely fond of scenes of resurrection. These occur, in one form or another, in *Anna Clayton*; *Myra* (her father, whom she had assumed dead, returns); *The Forsaken Bride* (the earl's supposedly drowned wife resurfaces as a teacher at his daughter's school); *Romance of the Republic* (the heroine's son, whom she had changed for another child in his cradle, and believed dead, is not); *The Discarded Daughter* (the heir, Lionel, survives a shipwreck; even more interestingly, the heroine's mother, when the girl arrives home to view the corpse, *revives* and they are able to spirit her away secretly so later she can frighten her evil husband to death!); *Marian Grey* (who turns up at first incognito five years after running from a loveless marriage and being presumed dead); *Allworth Abbey* (where two long lost daughters return to respectively delight and horrify their families); *Mary Derwent* (Catharine, Mary's mother, discovers she has *not* murdered her daughter); *Home Nook* (one heroine's husband is discovered to be alive just in time to prevent a bigamous marriage); *Lena Rivers* (the heroine is found by her father who had believed her to be—like her mother—dead); *Violet* (ditto); *Ernest Linwood* (ditto); and *Mary Derwent* (ditto).

This last seems an extraordinary pattern to find so frequently and elaborately developed. The father's role in a daughter's growing up has been supposedly that of promoting her independence and autonomy; if he is absent, of course, the daughter cannot do so. *These* fathers show up just in time to receive the displaced filial adoration of the young women in question. Gabriella, for example, "knows" her father: "I felt it, as if the voice of God had spoken from the clouds of heaven to proclaim it . . . the sacred name of

'Father.'" He responds, "My daughter! how sweet, how holy it sounds." (In her case, Lena's, and to a lesser extent, Violet's, this filial affection also *almost* precludes a marriage.)

A subtle analogy of this theme is the pervasive fantasy that the mother's spirit lives on in her daughter. Long before he can know for sure, Violet's father exclaims "do you know there are moments when I am . . . ready to believe that those holy eyes, that golden hair, those graceful movements, can belong only to my Violet's child?"; the same mysterious certainty is felt by mother's former lover and by grandfather in *Allworth Abbey*, while the "indefinable resemblance" of the Violet in *Nameless* torments the villain of the piece and a picture of her provokes another villain's suicide. Another potent picture appears in *Ernest Linwood*. Gabriella has found one of her mother as a girl: "I longed to kneel before it, to appeal to it, by every holy and endearing epithet,—to reach the cold, unconscious canvas, and cover it with my kisses and my tears." (Her companions notice the resemblance.)

We may add to this list the nearly fatal illnesses, precipitated by some separation or related trauma, that crowd the pages of these books, for the recovered heroine is usually compared to one "risen from the grave," reborn. A last form of resurrection is undergone by Gabriella's husband, whose depressions are followed by a mood that "is like life renewed—it is a resurrection from the dead,—it is a Paradise regained in the heart." The Paradise is of course created for him by his wife's forgiveness and love, restoring his self-esteem and trust. The issue is as fundamental as that; the ability to trust is notably missing in most of the characters in these novels, who appear to need the security of bonds forged across eternity.

The imperative to marry was very strong in 19th century America,[139] so that the daughter's need to break away fostered no less ambivalence than it does in our own time. However, ambivalence itself can serve to strengthen, through the spiral of denial and compensation, the mother–daughter bond. In such a case, the child will seek, even when grown up, a mother substitute— and we are back to the image, already fully illustrated in this chapter, of the childlike wife, and hence to the image of the husband as parent surrogate.[140] "Parents, never part with your children . . . . None but a mother's hand should rear her daughter . . . ." readers are warned in, for example, *The Mysterious Marriage*, and yet over and over in the group of books we are also treated to the spectacle of a girl being brought up properly by her future husband.

X. Themes of Salvation: The Guardian and Counselor

In discussing this theme, it is well to keep in mind that the mental image of the father is supposed to be constructed very much later than that of the mother. Moreover, the oedipal situation "is for a girl at least as much a mother–daughter concern as a father–daughter concern" because her pre-oedipal involvement with her mother is merely supplemented, so to speak, by an involvement with her father; it is not replaced, outgrown.[141] Therefore, presumably, what a girl learns from a father or father substitute will have a real-life, practical, practicable, even perhaps extra-domestic value for her; in Jungian terms, she will learn to work through the animus and come to terms with a guardian figure, so integrate those aspects of herself that the culture (or collective consciousness) terms "masculine." We have seen already that fathers fall into two groups in these stories: the absent fathers, and the persecutors, who force their daughters into loveless marriages. Each stereo-type reflects an aspect of mid-19th century social reality. The former is the more faithful image, of course, and with some modifications will be the popular fictional treatment of fathers for the century to follow. The latter is a brief melodramatic flare-up of a paternal mode that was definitely on the wane. Neither, clearly, provide much in the way of a model of the masculine. This may shed some light on the difficulties all these heroines have in integrating contrasexual behavior, but it is related to another incapacity of theirs, as well.

In the domestic sphere, the maternal role at mid-19th century and for decades thereafter was imbued with such power that it virtually precluded an equally significant relationship between daughters and fathers. A girl child can internalize the nurturant maternal role, and never get beyond it to the internalization of what some psychologists distinguish from maternality as "femininity," that is, heterosexual behavior.[142] I have already shown how very seldom such behavior (and it is not merely a question of portraying sexual misbehavior; it is a question of portraying even a mild hint of responsiveness) surfaces even in the "bad" women of these stories. At some point in her experience, in order to develop into a heterosexual being, a girl must have some encouragement from a man. How often is such encouragement—as opposed to exploitation, victimization, or a reverent adoration which is somewhat beside the point—depicted, in these books?

The two fathers who exercise a notable influence over their daughters in this group of texts are not much help. Violet Ross's real father (while ignorant that he is her real father) removes her as a child from the lowly circumstances in which he finds her, and rears her to be "perfect in every feminine grace and accomplishment"—though he becomes quickly bored with teaching her—and meanwhile provides her with whatever she desires. Violet grows up crushed with gratitude. Her father, in the old-fashioned way, attempts to coerce her into a loveless marriage, to maintain his total control over her, and is triumphant at her capitulation: "Papa Ross! I am yours! Do what you will with me!" (Though this sounds extreme, it is a fairly standard daughterly locution in these books; the difference is that it is usually the mother to whom such remarks are addressed.) The behavior of Papa Ross compares well with Violet's *foster* father's plan to have her abducted!

In *Mary Derwent's* early pages a mysterious Indian missionary, of "natural refinement of mind and manners," appears to teach Mary and her foster sister, imparting a "heavenly influence" to "the uppermost depths of her soul." It is much later in the story that she learns who he is. (Like Gabriella, she is not surprised. Both heroines are aided in this recognition by being able to compare the real, physically and spiritually beautiful father with another prospect, who is less so. Gabriella has been deceived by her father's evil twin, while Mary has her former foster father with whom to compare this scion of the British nobility.) Since Mary is too crippled to marry, she and her father live out their lives of benevolence together, leaving that romance's cast of characters incomplete. This characterization is the perfect model of the new "relatively democratic" father figure: remote, romantic, and ideal.

It is, however, not the good father but the potential husband who assumes most frequently the role of spiritual director in these books. Of these, Ellen's "brother" Johnny Humphrey and Beulah's guardian are the most notable examples, although throughout the period male characters in these stories arrange for orphan girls to be "perfected in accomplishment," and later marry them. John's sister introduces him to Ellen as "your brother as well as mine," and Ellen sees almost immediately that he is "a person to be feared." In the sense that Warner presumably intended, Ellen's fear is amply justified throughout the rest of the book, for John, like a personified superego rather than animus, manages to observe and comment on Ellen's every sin of omission and commission, and also to provide her with a searching and unrelenting course of religious instruction. At the story's end he still wants her to "do three things for him": write letters to him, read no novels, and—eventually—become his wife. Similarly, in Terhune's *Alone*, Ida receives a course of instruction from Morton Lacy, and, being older than Ellen, falls in love with him. Since he is committed elsewhere, Ida, after a period of bitter self-reproach—"he had tried to lead her, a wayward child, to the paths of happiness . . . . She had been impious enough to imagine that she was imbibing a fondness for holy things . . . ."—works out her own salvation in his absence. She is rewarded by his broken engagement, full explanations, and marriage to him. In *Mabel Vaughn*, the heroine also sets out to overcome a man's impression of her as worldly, by staying home from a European tour to re-form her brother Harry (who drinks), after the example of an invalid child, Little Rose. In this case, Mabel is rewarded some seven years after, by marriage to a much better man than the one to whom she set out to prove herself! The pattern of a child model persists: In *Agatha Lee's Inheritance*, the next door neighbor, destined for the church, urges the heroine (gently) to learn self-control and forsake worldliness. When she is rude to him, he reproaches her by saying that the little sister who was "laid under the violets... long ago" would never have spoken to him like that. Once Agatha has been ill for two weeks, learned to pray, and been given four years in which to amend her behavior, he proposes, and she remarks, upon accepting him, that "He will be near me just as of old—my guide, my counselor."

No guide nor counselor in these stories is more impressive than the heroine's mentor in Evans's *Beulah*. Dr. Guy Hartwell is explicitly not a Christian, though he impresses Beulah as "kinder and better" than most professing Christians she knows. This is the thin end of the wedge; the heroine's adolescence and early adulthood are animus-possessed, as she wrestles with the demons of religious Doubt and doubt of her guardian's love for her, in part because she refuses to acquiesce to any role of dependency until she has won back her religious Faith. (Here, the inability to trust is worked out on two levels; the human problem is perfectly paralleled in the religious symbolism.) Finally she is willing to tell him that she chooses him for a tyrant over "the tyrant Ambition," as he puts it. "Quick, *child*, decide!" [italics mine] She decides, and the novel closes with her at his feet, looking "reverently" up into his face, as she prepares to save *his* soul.

The proposition illustrated in this closing scene is stated in *Mary Derwent*: A woman's "safety lies in the very love which, though it make the bitterness of [her] life, is its safeguard, too." This is Catharine's advice to her child Tahmeroo—"Think not of your own rights too much; where struggling is sure to bring misery it is better to forbear." Her counsel is precisely that which the mothers of the two fictional heroes,[143] Ernest Linwood and St. Elmo Murry, offer to the heroines in these books. If a woman cannot perfect her manners and save her soul on the basis of a man's teachings, she can submit to his will. This will eventually teach her both the Christian and domestic virtues as a sort of inevitable by-product.

The question we are left with is whether any of these women have, directly or indirectly, been taught anything useful outside the domestic sphere, or a female role that is "feminine" rather than maternal. The overwhelming impression is that they have certainly not, unless one is willing to define an access of spirituality as transcending the values of domesticity (in this context, an untenable viewpoint), or unless one assumes that the married state in these fictions implies mature sexuality. Here also there are a number of reasons to reject such a view. Foremost is the "shrinking"—for example, Edna Earl faints at her wedding—that overcomes the childlike brides, but of equal importance is the simultaneous insistence on her maternal role toward her husband, and on her religious duty to marry. This last theme, of marriage as God's law, works also to support the function of the marriages in all these stories as a symbolic resolution and integration of all the intrapsychic conflicts and dramas in the earlier pages. To wed one's guardian and counselor, while one's shadow is redeemed and one's mother (if bad) eliminated or absorbed into oneself (if good), is indeed such a symbolic resolution. It is, however, one effected entirely within the terms not only of a patriarchial religion[144] but of a society in which *real* integration is prevented as effectually as the romance form prevents it in these books.[145]

XI. The Ties That Bind

The model of salvation as a regression to simple variations on parent–child relationships is underscored over and over in these books by a theme of almost-incest. When not marrying men they have always previously thought of as fathers or brothers, women nearly marry their brothers (*Violet*), spend years believing they have done so (*Allworth Abbey*), are suspected of infidelity when found embracing long-lost brothers (*The Forsaken Bride, Ernest Linwood*) or father (*Lena Rivers*). Such plot devices were by no means new to popular fiction of this period; indeed they formed a staple item in the French romances of previous centuries. Yet in this body of American fiction, so obsessively concerned with the fragmentation and re-creation of family relationships, such a plot formula is given new meaning. In the first place, incest was a favorite theme of the Romantic writers of the early and middle part of the century, including such Americans as Melville and Hawthorne. It was characteristic of the Romantic attitude to give new significance to what we would call unconscious desires. In the words of one commentator on the Romantics, "Their celebration of nature, the primitive, and the graveyards represented a longing for the tabooless pre-oedipal era."[146] We have seen that American women writers enjoyed a somewhat different repertoire of symbolic devices, to much the same end. In Jungian terms, however, both these women and the English Romantic poets may be seen as literary examples of the contrasexual self, as both employ the incest motif.

However, the ambivalences created in the pre-oedipal era (which is and was *not*, in our view, "tabooless"), rather than failed attempts at integration, inform the treatment of the incest theme in these women's books, depicting, as they do, an unprecedentedly binding and intimate sort of family tie. The incest taboo has two functions in any human society: It is a structural means of treating women as sexual property, and also a means of widening the network of human relations.[147] In these stories, the emphasis appears to fall on the former function. Invariably, the threat is discovered and removed—in order for a marriage to take place, *but also to reforge the family ties* that have been hidden by villainy or accidently broken. Heroines are placed within their families of origin and procreation, simultaneously. The first step beyond the pre-oedipal era of exclusive attachment to mother is the discovery that mother is unavailable *because she is father's property.*[148] All these stories attempt to undo that discovery. Whatever its difficulties, the pre-oedipal stage appears here as preferable to the girl child: secure mutual possession between women, in a sphere immediately or ultimately enclosed by masculine possession. To resolve the oedipal crisis, one must accept one's culture's sexual definition. To do this, a girl must rival her mother; clearly an impossibility in the world of these fictions. Obsessively, however, the possibility is entertained in all its horror. Incest serves, paradoxically, in these stories, to represent the ultimate horror of irretrievably broken family ties. When Violet reacts to the suggestion that she marry her brother, Edward (she loves him as a foster brother, and also intuitively senses that he is her real brother), she cries out in desolation, "'No father!—no brother!'" The threat of losing the established relationship is the source of her emotion, just as it is the source of Beulah's resistance to Dr. Hartwell's (unfatherly) love, and of Lena's resistance to recognizing an obvious relationship. But scenes of loss involving heterosexual relations pale beside the behavior of Alma and the mother who believes her a child of incest. "'Mamma, will you not embrace me for this once in our lives?' pleaded Alma, holding out her arms. 'Go! go! go! go, girl, and leave me. Is this the advantage you would take of the very first visit I permit you to my presence?'" And later this mother speaks a word "which must sever [Alma] at once and forever from [her lover] and from all others" (*Allworth Abbey*). As an illustration of the most terrible infantile fantasies of the mother, and hence of the dynamics of pre-oedipal ambivalence, this particular pair of characters has no peer.

Another fictional device for dramatizing the horror of broken family ties is that threat, or suspicion, of bastardy. This theme crops up in *The Discarded Daughter, The Mysterious Marriage, Hope Leslie, Mary Derwent, Lena Rivers, Little Sunshine, Myra, Nameless,* and *The Forsaken Bride.* No heroine is, naturally, marriageable until she is sure she is legitimate. Again, the removal of this threat, of having been born out of wedlock (of having been abandoned by father, mother, or both) enables the removal of the threat of spinsterhood. Two sets of family ties are forged for Lena, for example: The girls who actually are illegitimate, such as Leone in *Little Sunshine*—"Oh my mother! my mother! Oh, God, can such things be?"—commit suicide.

Social isolation, to be abandoned, to be "alone!", perceived in whatever terms, is portrayed as the worst of fates, the worst of fears. It is not only alienation from the rest of normal humanity, but, in the case of these heroines, from the self—for sense of self, as we have seen, is depicted as dependent on replication of the mother, of relatedness personified. Needless to say, in the attributes of the idealized mother, her innocence, her self-sacrificial devotion and service, her ability to invest home and family with spiritual values, there is an enormous fantasy component, as a necessary balance to the terror of inner emptiness in the daughter who loses that inner ideal image. There is no way to attain selfhood in the world depicted.

This body of fiction, as we have seen, shows few opportunities and many dangers in the path of any young woman who does not want to "be mother." Work outside the home debilitates and corrupts. Fathers provide no support for independence or achievement in their daughters. Daughters are not allowed to relate to them or to other males in a heterosexual rather than a maternal way; indeed, these heroines either shrink from other males, or project the maternal image onto them. The world of this fiction is truly a woman's world, homebound, and bounded by the ideology of woman's spiritual mission. These stories were popular from the 1840s for more than a decade after the Civil War.[149] Women's fiction was never again to portray quite such exclusivity.[150] Between that period and the rise of the story of romantic suspense in the 1950s there was in fact no comparable body of homogeneous fiction, and yet each dynamic, each topic here explored, remained viable material in the hands of women writing for women.

The Texts

Page numbers of important references to these texts, as they appear in sequence in this chapter, follow each bibliographical citation.

Briggs, Emily E. *Ellen Parry, or Trials of the Heart.* New York: D. Appleton and Co., 1850. (38, 17)

Chesebro, Caroline. *Amy Carr; or, The Fortune Teller.* New York: M.W. Dood, 1864. (172)

Child, Lydia Maria. *Romance of the Republic.* Boston: Ticknor and Fields, 1867. (188)

Cummins, Maria Susanna. *Mabel Vaughn.* Boston: Houghton, Mifflin and Co., 1885. (1857)

Douglas, Amanda M. *Home Nook; or, The Crown of Duty.* Boston: Lee and Shephard, 1873. (225)

Downing, Fanny. *Nameless.* Raleigh, North Carolina: William B. Smith and Co., 1865. (16, 19, 193, 208–209, 57, 231)

Downs, Sarah F. *The Forsaken Bride.* New York: G. W. Dillingham, 1886. (1881)

Evans, Augusta Jane. *Beulah.* New York: A. L. Burt Company. (n.d.) (1859) (65, 116–117, 339–340, 355, 202, 431, 440)

———. *St. Elmo.* New York: Carleton, Publisher, 1867. (436, 528, 531)

Gilman, Caroline. *Love's Progress.* New York: Harper, 1840. (40, 57, 58, 126, 164, 171)

Hentz, Caroline Lee. *Eoline; or, Magnolia Vale.* Philadelphia: T. B. Peterson and Brothers, 1869. (1852) (29, 56, 61, 112, 115, 74–75, 260, 216–218)

———. *Ernest Linwood.* Boston: John P. Jewett and Co., 1856. (32, 319, 81, 327, 329, 230, 333–334, 257, 430–431, 286, 287)

————. *Rena; or, The Snowbird.* Philadelphia: T. B. Peterson and Brother, 1851. (27, 40, 16, 144, 18, 147, 232, 34, 136)

Higham, Mary R. *Agatha Lee's Inheritance.* New York: Anson D. F. Randolph and Company, 1878. (103, 138, 207)

Holmes, Mary J. *Lena Rivers.* New York: AMS Press, Inc., 1870. (1856) (45, 349)

————. *Marian Grey.* New York: J. H. Sears and Co. (n.d.) (1863)

Howard, Adah M. *Little Sunshine; or, The Secret of the Death Chamber.* New York: Norman L. Munro, 1886. (162, 130, 132)

Lee, Hannah. *Elinor Fulton.* Boston: Whipple and Damrell, 1837. (41, 39, 104, 130, 138)

McIntosh, Maria Jane. *Emily Herbert; or, The Happy Home.* New York: D. Appleton and Co., 1854.

————. *Violet; or, The Cross and the Crown.* Boston: John P. Jewett and Co., 1856. (108, 402, 155, 312, 120, 340, 45, 194, 193)

Moore, Mrs. H. J. *Anna Clayton; or, The Mother's Trial.* Boston: Crown and Co., 1857. (1855) (21, 109, 171, 303, 310)

Parton, Sara Payson. *Ruth Hall, A Domestic Tale of the Present Time.* New York: Mason Brothers, 1855. (39, 49, 331)

Sedgwick, Catharine Maria. *Home.* Boston: James Munroe and Co., 1835. (13–14)

————. *Hope Leslie; or, Early Times in The Massachusetts.* New York: White, Gallaher and White, 1827. (24)

Sigourney, Lydia H. *Lucy Howard's Journal.* New York: Harper and Brothers, 1858. (84, 111, 313, 232, 63, 322, 93, 261, 308)

Southworth, E.D.E.N. *The Discarded Daughter.* Philadelphia: T. B. Peterson and Brothers, 1875. (1852) (34, 56–57, 320–324, 378)

————. *Allworth Abbey.* New York: F. M. Lupton, 1876. (1865) (114–115, 345, 381, 416, 215, 248–250, 278, 421, 250, 278)

Stephens, Ann S. *Mary Derwent.* Philadelphia: T. B. Peterson and Brothers, 1858. (388–389, 116–117, 344, 42–44, 59, 63, 382, 404, 85, 15, 325)

————. *Myra: the Child of Adoption.* New York: Irwin P. Beadle and Co., 1860. (1856) (10–11, 23, 31)

Terhune, Mary Virginia. *Alone.* Richmond, Virginia: A. Morris, 1854. (7, 21, 381, 225)

————. *The Hidden Path.* New York: J. C. Derby, 1855. (30–31, 58, 62, 120, 132–133, 231, 222, 281, 313–314, 387–388, 433–434)

Ward, Catherine G. *The Mysterious Marriage; or, The Will of My Father.* New York: William Burnett, 1834. (298, 133, 385)

Warner, Susan. *The Wide Wide World.* New York: George P. Putnam, 1852. (vol. I, 84–89; vol. II, 81–82; vol. I, 76; vol. II, 327)

4

A DREAM OF PLACE:
Into the 20th Century

I. The Home Invaded

By the end of the 19th century, domestic fiction, as a genre, was no longer written. Examples, good and bad, were still being published, but so were several new forms of women's fiction. None dominated the market, nor created a new genre—until the 1950s, with the advent of the novel of romantic suspense, sometimes called the "new gothic." This chapter deals with that period of fragmentation.

Histories of women in America regularly mention one factor in social change, the effects wars have had on woman's role. "Next to the slave," Lerner states, "no group in society was more deeply affected by the Civil War than were American women," who, North and South, took on nontraditional jobs.[151] In the three decades that followed, social change occurred on many levels, each change affecting women's lives profoundly. The United States became modern: a predominantly urban nation dramatically altered in appearance by immigrant groups and by an increasingly conspicuous cleavage between rich and poor. This was to have a significant impact on how the American family saw itself.[152] Mass production changed work opportunities for both men and women, indeed, the nature of work itself, and began to introduce technology of all sorts into the home.[153]

Well before 1900, as we have seen, women had entered the industrial and commercial work world. By the opening of the 20th century they had at least some place in virtually all professions and most occupations. The overwhelming majority of white working women were young and single, and left their jobs for home when they married.[154] But it was not the Home of the mid-19th century to which they returned. By the turn of the century, the values of corporate efficiency and rationality were already remolding the concept of the home. Following the Civil War, standards of efficiency had been urged upon housewives in the popular manuals of housekeeping by women, for women. The concept of the *professional housewife*—and mother —took hold.[155] The reformers of the Progressive Era of the early 20th century took much that had been private into the public realm, in their desire to save society through moderate changes. The family became the locus of their most far-reaching efforts, and the rationalized middle-class family which acknowledged the advice of experts became increasingly the "norm."

Not least among these reformers were the women whose "primary concern was service to others and to society, as contrasted with feminists whose primary object was the achievement of individual opportunities for women."[156] Carl Degler shows in detail how middle-class married women throughout the last decades of the 19th century and the early decades of the 20th expanded their activities beyond the home, to make a Home of the whole society.[157] From church work and settlement work to the WCTU (1874) and the Women's Trade Union League (1903), these women and their daughters brought the new gospel of a *better* Home to America.

The contradiction is obvious. In the years before World War I, for women, the ideal of self-fulfillment rather than living for others gained ground. Ironically, this new "right" was still supposed to be best realized in the home. Improvements in education or working conditions for women were premised upon this idea, whatever other effects they had. Degler is of the opinion, in fact, that suffrage succeeded only when the appeal to individual rights as its basis was abandoned, for the new justification that women had a special contribution to make to society, "from their character as women—as wives and mothers, as homemakers."[158]

In the Progressive Era the rights and interests of the child were given an unprecedented importance. Child-study and innovations in education, such as kindergartens, and John Dewey's concept of the "child-centered school," were rapidly popularized and implemented.[159] Business and the state began to take over such other traditional functions of the family as recreation, health, and insurance. In a nation always at least half-committed to change, accepting these newly offered "opportunities" came easily. Yet, again, there was an inherent contradiction. While mothers welcomed the help of the new helping professions, they began to feel more and more uneasy about their own abilities as parents. Ward's 1902 *Confessions of a Wife* already portrays a wife and mother who is totally dependent on her doctor in both roles.

However, this new image of maternity as a learned technique, in need of expert advice, is no more significant from our point of view than the new image of wifeliness which accompanies it. A revolution in morals was well underway by 1900, and World War I and the rebellion of the 1920s helped it on its way.[160] The changes that World War I brought about for women, then, were not really changes in work opportunities, although the boost that war and victory gave to the American economy had decisive effects for families and women.[161] The real change was toward the image of woman as man's companion, moving more freely in his world and sharing more of his interests, jokes, and amusements than her mother ever had. A novel such as Norris's *Mother* (1912) already reflects the new image of worldly sophistication: It is a prewar novel, and the heroine ends by rejecting such new ideas. After World War I, this component of wifeliness is simply included. The American revolt against "Puritan" or "Victorian" repressiveness, particularly sexual repressiveness, also antedated the war but was hardly set back by it. This revolt took place in new urban communities, seeking for an order[162] no longer found in the vanishing, rural, small town world where Norris's Mother bore and raised her eight children. Twentieth-century woman was to be cosmopolitan, civilized, and fulfilled.

Yet once again a contradiction is present. As the 1920s came to a close, it seemed to contemporary observers that the tide had turned against all ideas of individual opportunity for women. Ironically, the new search for sexual satisfaction led women "where the old denials of sexual drives had also led: to marriage, a family, and total responsibility for child and home care."[163] Moreover, women were not complaining about this. They became disillusioned with the very ideals of economic independence and exciting work, partly because sexual love made marriage, at least, more desirable to them. "We are tired of our rights, give us our privileges again," went the popular plea.[164]

Throughout the early decades of the 20th century, then, the great majority of white working women left work to marry and to raise children. (It was not until World War II, which was longer and demanded greater productivity than World War I, that women's employment was significantly changed.)[165] And, according to one writer, by 1930 the invasion of the helping professions had already seriously eroded the capacity of the family to socialize or care for its younger members.[166] Their socialization, at any rate, had begun to take place elsewhere—and not just at school.

The proliferation of advertising spread the consumer ideology throughout the culture, but that ideology was already present in embryo by the turn of the century. The desire for money-making work outside the home and for sexual freedom were stimulated by the new availability of labor-saving devices and cheap pretty clothes.[167] In Wilkins/Freeman's *The Portion of Labor*

(1901) a young daughter of the working class found in a department store "the very breath of all the mysterious joy and hitherto untasted festivity of this earth into which she had come. She felt deep in her childish soul the sense of a promise of happiness in the future, of which this was a foretaste." And her poor father felt already the discomfort that was to characterize the American parent for the time to follow: "Her little desires seemed to him the most important and sacred needs in the whole world. He watched her with pity and admiration, and shame at his own impotence of love to give her all."

The new affluence of the 1920s, the spread of mass culture, further encouraged Americans to depend on material rather than moral standards of worth. The private sphere was no longer the locus of value, either in the present, or for the future. Fathers and mothers both lost authority. Mothers in this whole body of fiction are dull traditionalists at best, while the fragmentation of the self of the young heroine is drastically redefined, as early as the 1890s, by conflicts between her maternal and sexual needs, as well as her desires for worldly success. "The authority of industry was being drawn as a sustaining father figure while the traditional arenas of social intercourse . . . were pictured as decrepit, threatening, and basically incapable of providing any level of security."[168] We will see what becomes of the heroine who turns to *this* new authority figure in her search for security: She becomes a wife and mother, it is true, but not without difficulties.

The increased mobility of Americans also loosened women's attachment to traditional domestic values. On a closed frontier, spanned by the railways, the cult of true womanhood was no longer needed, neither as civilizing mission nor as escape from extraordinary outdoor labors.[169] The pain of parting from Home became less dire, as new and simpler homes became easier to establish and to visit. For the first time since the early national period, travel outside the continental United States began to figure largely in women's fiction: Burnett's best-selling 1907 romance, *The Shuttle*, takes its title from the new availability of rapid and comfortable transatlantic transportation.

The invasion of the home, then, was mounted by the economy, the state, and a climate of ideas that combined Darwin, Freud, some European modernism, and our own optimistic and materialistic belief in inevitable progress. Women asked for, and got, a new definition of family, and a new complexity in the number and nature of roles they might choose to fill. At the same time, and by the same forces, the genre of domestic fiction was broken up into fragments, and women's fiction became definable only in terms of a persistent interest in the images of Mother, Mother's Daughter, and Home. In the pages that follow, we will examine stories in which heroines, far from enjoying new freedoms, suffer under a multiplicity of new demands and pressures—and eventually succumb to them.

II. The Genre Invaded

For 50 years, the imagery of Mother, Daughter, and Home persists: in historical romances, regional fiction, girls' books,[170] sensation novels,[171] mysteries, novels good and bad—books which undoubtedly appealed to men as well as women. This chapter deals with texts that were selected either because their writers wrote best-sellers (as in the cases of Barclay, Deland, Rinehart, Stratton-Porter, Atherton, Wiggin, Daviess, Norris, Winsor, Bailey, Barnes), or because their writers had, and in some cases are still having, long, prolific, profitable careers writing to one or two formulas of their own. Some careers, of course, illustrate both criteria (as in the cases of Loring, Norris, Baldwin, Hill, Slottman, Duffield, Gaddis, and others). Some books are seriously literary, while dealing with the persistent themes in question (Brown's, Wilkins/Freeman's, Canfield/Fisher's). I am aware that such judgments will not please everyone; they do not entirely please me. The fact is that fashions in "serious" literature date more rapidly than those in "popular" fiction, so that some quite solemn novels of the 1920s, for example, are so topical that they make duller and more meaningless reading, now, than—say—the luridly sentimental *Stella Dallas*, which is a powerfully archetypal production.

This chapter deals with the years in which literature became "modern." Literary modernism is not an issue relevant to this study, however, since none of these books departs noticeably from 19th century traditions of characterization, historical continuity, and "realistic" detail, a style which calls no attention to itself. In other words, these women are writing romances with all the trappings of literary realism. Moreover, as I have already suggested, their themes are the same themes popular in women's fiction, although with some differences of emphasis which we will explore.

This heterogeneous collection of texts, then, takes us from 1885 to 1950, to the dawn of the genre of romantic suspense fiction. Mothers and daughters and homes in this collection of books, at the mercy of the industrial state, Madison Avenue, the social sciences, and Hollywood, are nevertheless recognizably of the same families we have already read about.

III. The Self Invaded

In the years before 1910, the mass media and modern advertising had not yet consolidated American ideas of woman and her place, as they were soon to do.[172] Yet themes in women's fiction of the period show that the 20th century media creation of woman as sex object and status symbol is underway. First of these new themes is a new concern with personal appearance, in which natural endowments and their embellishment by hairdressing, clothing, and even cosmetics no longer serve merely as indicators of (bad) moral quality. In the domestic novel cleanliness was, of course, godly—but so also was simplicity. Beyond lay the perils of worldliness. Hence a heroine's hair might escape its bounds to indicate her closeness to the Romantic ideal of nature, while the shadow figure's hair was tortured by fashionable art.

Mary Wilkins/Freeman's novel, *By the Light of the Soul* (1907), provides a transitional example of a new self-consciousness about fashion in fictional heroines. The child Maria "felt vain, but she was sorry because of her vanity. She knew how charming her pink gingham gown was, but she knew that she ought to have asked her mother if she might wear it . . . . She had put [it] on . . . on account of Wollaston Lee . . . . The pink gingham was as the mating plumage of a bird." To portray such an ambivalence of attitude sympathetically is quite new. In the same novel, a part of the "terrible" accusations leveled against the stepmother villainess of the piece is "You have not even loved [your own child] Evelyn. You have only got her nice clothes. You have never loved her . . . . You are not made right." Yet Maria, the accuser, has all along taken pleasure (sometimes a whole page in its description) in her own "nice clothes," and throughout the novel it is prettiness that is assumed to be the issue of value between girls and men.

In Elizabeth Stuart Phelps Ward's *Confessions of a Wife* (1902), the heroine has a favorite, ruby-colored dressing gown: Her husband "likes me in this gown. He likes the lace, and he likes the color. He says it is the shade of my ruby [wedding ring]." When the marriage has all but failed, and wife is about to make a last great scene, she arrays herself in her "old ruby gown" for the attempt, later wondering if he'll come home if she wears it. Here the issue is fashionable attractiveness—but complicated by the issue of vanishing youth and the desire to recapture it—a theme to be dealt with later.

In Gene Stratton-Porter's *A Girl of the Limberlost* (1910) the mother of the indomitable heroine Elnora is portrayed as cruelly withholding from her daughter the money for proper school clothes. The consequent mockery of her peers is too much for even Elnora's courage. A whole chapter is devoted to a description of a friendly neighbor's shopping expedition to outfit her properly. Furthermore, we are only sure that Elnora's mother is truly purged of her hatred for her daughter (whose birth, in a unique twist of a plot, caused her *father's* death) when she, the mother, bleaches her suntan, goes to a hairdresser, buys stylish clothes, and tastefully furnishes a house in town.

In Margaret Sangster's *Janet Ward: A Daughter of the Manse* (1902), a college student says that "even more than anyone else, a Christian woman should be attractive in outward seeming. Miss Prescott [the evangelist] influences many girls here who would not notice her if she were not fine in her carriage and smart in her dress," and throughout the novel the garb of the heroine and her friends is described in pleasurable detail. In Grace Livingston Hill's 1903 novel, *According to the Pattern*, her heroine attempts to become fashionable, but learns better, and becomes a simple Baptist. Later heroines of Hill's never need to make this difficult choice, but acquire expensive clothes while keeping the faith. The heroine of Harrison's *A Bachelor Maid* (1894) is contrasted with her villainous stepmother in that, *having* "mere externals" such as stockings of "fine black silken openwork, [and] high-heeled slipper[s] of patent leather, with a small buckle of brilliants," she can gracefully take them for granted—while the shadow, being deprived, pursues her course of deception and manipulation in order to acquire just such things.

In her (1944) *Psychology of Women* Helene Deutsch writes, of the adolescent narcissism which persists in women who continue dependent on their mothers, "Every gesture, every inner and outer experience, is put before the mother and subjected to her . . . criticism. In some cases this dependence remains fixed on the mother, more often it is transferred to others. The happiness or unhappiness of a person with such an attachment depends absolutely on the judgment of others, and she expends a great deal of energy in finding out the reactions of those around her to everything she does."[173] This is the personality type these women's fictions have just begun to describe: young women, essentially dependent and passive, who derive most of their sense of self-worth from the appearance that they are able to present to others. With the right clothes comes complete social validation from other women as well as from men. A pubescent competitiveness about just the right, fashionable ingredients of prettiness is retained into what passes for adulthood, and that prettiness is unconsciously needed so badly that shadow figures are often embodiments of that need satisfied by nearly criminal means.

The 1920s did not begin the search for glamour. The icon of the sexy flapper, while more serviceable to the economy than the icon of the pure mother, was not in the long run as useful as a combination of the two—the image of the wife as sexual companion to her husband.[174] This image is in fiction by the turn of the century; such books as *Confessions of a Wife* (1902) and *Margaret Warrener* (1901) depict women who are as romantically and sexually dependent on their husbands' love and attention as any heroine of the 1920s or after. Yet in the women's books published between 1910 and 1950, the descriptive power devoted to aids to feminine attractiveness, like the business of advertising, increases enormously. The fantasy of a Whole New Expensive Wardrobe becomes a regular feature, exhibited in Hill's *Crimson Roses* (1928) and *Ladybird* (1930), Prouty's *Stella Dallas* (1928), Norris's *Heartbroken Melody* (1938), Lee's *Tabloid Love* (1936), and Brucker's *Together* (1945). (Sometimes it occurs in symbolic form, as when Dee in *So Deep My Love* (1944) marries a rich man, who doesn't want her to resume her carreer but gives her a gold vanity case.) These wardrobes are not necessarily or even usually trousseaux, but their function of conferring sexual acceptability is similar. They appear regularly with a new and rather more sinister fictional convention that I call the "mirror stare."

IV. The Self in the Mirror

If Lasch is (as I think) correct in claiming that "modern advertising seeks to promote not so much self-indulgence as self-doubt,"[175] thereby capitalizing on and consolidating the effects of mother–daughter dependencies, a glance in the mirror should reassure none of our heroines. Nor does it. Here is one of Hill's heroines on the eve of marriage: "She looked into the eyes in the glass to see whether she could find any trace of the woman that was to be, out of the self she was. Was it possible for her to fulfill the great ideal of the man who had chosen her out of all the world to be his wife?" (*Crimson Roses*); and, later, "Oh, it was all a mistake, a dreadful mistake. She was just a plain little common girl, and she could never be a rich man's wife."

In story after story, the heroine observes her mirrored image and gives some variant on the cry: "That Jeffrey . . . should have chosen her!" (*Empty Arms*); what's "wonderful" is that "*Drew* loves her" (*Silver Slippers*); "Paul Cartwright loved her . . . Paul Cartwright, rich and popular and important" (*Heartbroken Melody*); "How could he love her? It was a miracle . . . How had she looked to him? Had she been lovely in his eyes? She tried to see herself in the mirror in the positions he had seen. Awful!" (*To-morrow Morning*). "In my heart," one young woman confesses, "I felt it was my fault [that I lost Rix]. That I hadn't been desirable—enough; because I couldn't keep him . . . something must have been lacking in me . . . . It made me uncertain, insecure" (*You Can't Escape*); and, "Would Jim like her?" (*Together*). Another young woman in this story fails to recognize her transformed-by-love self in the mirror. "Oh darling, I just can't get used to the idea that I'm the girl you really love" (*The Shelf Full of Dreams*). "The only mirror that counts anyway," broods the heroine of Winsor's *Star Money*, after examining herself, "is the look in a man's eyes. That expression . . . seemed the most valuable gift she could ever receive."

This transfer of a sense of identity and worth to "mere externals," including the "admiration, attention, expressed flattery" (*One Woman's Story*) of a man, is symbolized most strikingly in the famous closing scene of *Stella Dallas*, where the self-sacrificing (but crude, tasteless, and unattractive) mother has given up her beautiful daughter in order that she may have parents whose appearance will do her credit. Stella stands outside the ballroom window, on the night of Laurel's debut, and "The clear plate glass with the light beyond it was a perfect mirror. Laurel gave herself a long look. Six feet away Stella caught that look . . . . It wasn't meant for her . . . . It was like catching a bit of shooting star," and Stella waits for a glimpse of the "young god who had made Laurel look at herself like that." It is no longer only an idealized Mother's judgment of the self that is relevant. Now it is an equally fantastic idealization of oneself by a man that matters.[176]

In 1910, when Barclay wrote the best seller *The Rosary*, more than stylishness or sexiness could be seen in a woman. "My vision of her," claims the (blinded) hero "followed the inspired order of things—spirit, soul, and body. Her spirit was so pure and perfect, her soul so beautiful, noble, and womanly, that the body which clothed soul and spirit partook of their perfection . . . ." Yet even this heroine believes herself too plain to be beloved, and consequently behaves in a most frustrating fashion, until, in Chapter 29 (entitled "Jane Looks into Love's Mirror") she sees the paintings this man painted of her before he lost his sight. By 1928, remarks about spirit or soul are replaced, if alluded to at all, by the suggestion that heroines are perfectly "tasteful" and "fine" throughout, somehow. In *Silver Slippers*, the hero exclaims, "You belong to beautiful things, not to serviceable ones," and "I want your loveliness untouched by serviceable things"; while, in *Heartbroken Melody*, the heroine is equally confused by the "important" Paul Cartwright: "Ah, it's going to be thrilling . . . to be always correctly dressed and at the right places," Honor says. "He told me once that I was a 'career woman.' I'm not sure what it means . . . . But I feel as if I were one. I mean destined to travel and know people, and live through changes and excitements."

The first change that Honor survives is a crippling accident. Paul visits. "She knew that her hair was tumbled and her face shiny and unpowdered . . . . She drew the folds of an old kimono across her breast. Her whole world revolved about her in a very sickness of realization." Obviously, Paul is lost to her. By this new ideal of sexual attractiveness, women are separated from each other; divided against one another, in fact. *Paul goes back to his wife.* Daughters like Stella's Laurel, and like Honor, cease, consciously, to model themselves upon their mothers; they experience themselves instead in competition with all other women.

As Showalter describes it, the 19th century restriction on heterosexual relationships endowed women not only with their supposed spiritual beauty and superiority, but with a motive to avoid marriage,[177] rather than seek it desperately as the only validation of self. This was useful in pursuing a career, and perhaps not so lonely a course in an era that did *not* restrict homosocial relationships. As Sheila Rothman observes, "The ideal wife-companion had little time left for anything apart from her marital relationship . . . . Female fellowship was a victim of romantic marriage."[178]

V. The Wife in the Mirror: Her Father over Her Shoulder

The new "sexual freedom" of the 20th century, then, paradoxically put women in the position of needing more than ever to fulfill masculine ideals of women. Inevitably, a component of their new role was *imitation of men*. (When, in the 1950s, sociologists made the comparison with minority groups, this copying of the so-called superior group was recognized.)[179] The flapper herself, for all her sexiness, was "a good sport, and a pal," devaluing women's interests and preferring the company of men at work and play. Yet this sort of young woman is not often a heroine in women's fiction.

Dinnerstein puts it this way: *"The essential fact about paternal authority, the fact that makes both sexes accept it as a model for the ruling of the world, is that it is under prevailing conditions a sanctuary from maternal authority"* [author's emphases].[180] On no other assumption can we explain how the men who are depicted by women's fiction from 1885 to the 1920s would make *anyone* want to identify with them. True, they are no longer the harsh patriarchs or careless losers of young wives and infants that crowded the pages of earlier books. Yet it is hard to see them as a positive influence. The father figures of *Ruth the Outcast* (1897), *Violet Lisle* (1892), and *Sweet Danger* (1902) are definitely misogynists. Violet's father, meeting her again after she has been a year on her own, claims our attention by commenting mildly, "I am glad you were not a chorus girl, dear." (She has only been a singer.)

The father figures in the fiction of Wilkins/Freeman, Harrison, and Sangster hardly illustrate the new "relatively democratic" father figure, for they are portrayed as clearly inferior beings. The fathers in *The Portion of Labor* and *By the Light of Soul* are wholly dependent upon the good (or bad) sense and management of their wives. After her mother's death, Maria's father remarries—a woman whose beauty is barely skin deep. The stepmother's hard selfishness eventually drives him to death, from overwork and anxiety over debts. In a political argument, the father in *Pembroke* orders his daughter's betrothed out of the house forever; he does not return for a decade. What is really best described as a stubborn male stupidity is also a feature in *A Bachelor Maid* where the heroine has, in observing her father, "learned to look upon man as an oppressor of woman; to mistrust him as morally weak when physically most attractive; to resent the domestic law-giver; to dread giving up liberty. . . ." But the heroine cannot draw a general conclusion, only a personal one. When he, like Maria's father and others, is duped by an evil woman, and she "sees his full childishness . . . something within her . . . asked . . . whether, in the happy natural estate of girlhood and wifehood, where the relations with father and husband, or other so-called 'governing' power of home, are as they should be, this modern unrest and impatience of women are to be found." By story's end, she is willing to try making a home "as it should be," and we expect her to succeed better than the weak invalid mother who died when she was 12. The father in *Janet Ward*, a pastor, will "never grow old," and is "loveable, loving, impulsive, pinning his faith to the possibilities of tomorrow . . . though no further along in the path of what men of the world call success, than he had been at twenty-three." The fathers in *Ladybird* and *A Girl of the Limberlost* are, respectively, criminal and adulterous.

Fathers, in other words, are not reliable authority figures in women's fiction of the turn of the century, any more than they could be considered so in the rapidly changing social world. Mothers are another matter, for at least until the middle of the 1920s they are most frequently portrayed as having quite a firm grip on essential realities, far better able to control situations than men. In contrast, the new untrustworthiness of men bears none of the power of projected fantasy borne by the rakes or the guardian heroes of the 19th century. Men are children, and continue so in women's popular fiction through World War II. Duped, weak, vain and vainglorious, selfish and petty, failures in business and human relationships because of their poor judgment or vicious habits, unfaithful, greedy, mother-dominated, insensitive, or simply silly, they throng the pages of best-seller and formula fiction alike.

The bad fathers of the 1920s–1940s are, unsurprisingly, absent fathers, often because they have died, but also because they have abdicated their role, as in *The Promises of Alice, Stella Dallas, The Heart's Kingdom,* or *A Daughter of the Vine.* In the 1930s and after, they are not even able to veto the maternal power that constrains their daughters' lives to conformity (*Joretta, Too Young to Marry*). This picture hardly conflicts with the larger social picture, in which authority is taken from the individual and transferred elsewhere—to the state, schools, corporations, and their advertising.

Yet the problem of authority for women, as Dinnerstein has reminded us, is not only a social question. "Woman cannot and should not separate herself from the Mother [archetype] as man must; her freedom lies in her increasing consciousness of how this image lives itself within her own psyche. She must perceive not only its duality but also its archetypal unity if she is to see the wholeness of herself." This Jungian's formulation of "object relations" emphasizes the particular difficulty inherent in a girl's separation and individuation processes. Only the child who can establish the good mother securely in the inner world and therefore perceive others and herself as whole can work through the depressive position. The ability to identify with a good father follows.[181] However, if she has one, "the mother's man-hating shadow," continues Wickes, "may separate the growing child from love and trust in the father who is the first image of man,"[182] and hence interfere with her independent development. We began to see examples of this situation in the domestic fiction of the mid-19th century, considerably disguised, however, by the submissive and "all-forgiving" qualities of the ideal woman. *These* mothers, in contrast, are hardly all-forgiving, and seem actively to discourage their daughters from trusting or identifying with any masculine qualities. (This issue is separate from but joined to the newly overt sexual jealousy between 20th century mothers and daughters, which serves to provoke "femininity.") In the earlier fiction, heroines simply failed to develop those qualities that identification with a present, positive father figure helps to develop. In this later period, heroines appear to be in worse case, for they develop, at an unconscious and hence self-destructive level, reverse images of their potential independence and achievement.

Jungian psychology does not speak of identification with a role model, but of the recognition and integration of various inherent qualities or behavior patterns. The contrasexual elements of the self are conceived of in terms of broad cultural stereotypes; thus, the anima's positive quality of consciousness is diffuse, while that of the animus is focused. The animus may play a very negative role in a girl's or a woman's mental life, for this focus can easily be turned into irrelevancies, especially conventional ideas and opinions.[183] This negative animus may result in a woman remaining imprisoned in the routine details of her existence, "shutting her into a smaller and smaller space,"[184] neglecting the "feminine" principle of relatedness. This is especially likely to happen if a girl has been informed by her father that she could not do something independently[185]—or if her *mother's* negative animus has told them *both* this.

Moreover, the negative animus may be projected onto the man in a woman's life, for often, even if "there is no man on the outside to torture her, the woman would get it from within, for when she is alone her animus assures her that she is lonely and nobody and nothing and will never get anywhere." In the case of projection, she is mired in misplaced pity for the man who fits her fantasy of "destructive dwarf."[186] If a woman's father has appeared to her mother to be a destructive dwarf, she is likely to see him that way herself; to construct a negative self-image, and to be unable to achieve autonomy. She will have trouble focussing her mind or energy on independent creative work, because she will—at least some of the time believe that she should not, and cannot, anyway.

Such a pattern surfaces quite clearly from the books examined in this chapter. Woman after woman has not only transferred her dependency to a fiancé or husband, and moreover to a husband whom, in a parody of practical strength, she pities and tolerates while he falls in love with other women (*Margaret Warrener, Cecily, You Can't Escape, The Labyrinth, Stella Dallas, Heartbroken, Sweet Danger*); drinks, dopes (*Confessions*); loses money, jobs and self respect (*To-morrow Morning, Too Young To Marry, A Prince Came Riding*); rapes her (*Three Nights of Love, The Hundredth Chance*); uses his pride to make her suffer for years (*Pembroke, K., By the Light of The Soul, The Street of Seven Stars, The Mistress of Shenstone, The Shuttle, Together*); or is merely an insufferable, insensitive boor forcing her into the most conventional of roles (*Amazing Interlude, Joretta, Silver Slippers, So Deep My Love, White Collar Girl, The Glass House, One Woman's Story, Secret Marriage, Pretty Polly*). Repeatedly, heroines allow themselves to be distracted or deflected from careers by these relationships (*The Glass House, Margaret Warrener, You Can't Escape, To-morrow Morning, Labyrinth, Cecily, So Deep My Love*).

When, rarely, fathers are portrayed as having some remnant of a value structure to impart to their female children, it is because of their unconventionality. For example, in Stratton-Porter's *Her Father's Daughter* (1921), the heroine Linda claims "I am exactly like Father," who tries to make up for having provided her with a frivolous, selfish, and deceitful stepmother by teaching her natural history. The symbol of her identification is the low-heeled shoes he approves of! Her inability, finally, to identify with her *real* mother, who died after her birth, is a far more significant plot element. In *The Shuttle*, a father is portrayed who deviates from the stereotype of businessman enough to say, "If you were a son instead of a daughter, I should see I might have confidence in you . . . . Your notes and sketches and summing up of probable costs [on the estate to be rebuilt] did us both credit—I say 'both' because your business education is the result of our long talks and journeyings together." Taking a 12-year old girl to visit mines and railroads, one gathers, was hardly the usual thing.

The apotheosis of the unconventional and (in the usual sense) impractical father appears in Canfield/Fisher's best-selling novel *The Homemaker* (1924), in which the father and mother exchange roles after he loses his job and is later crippled in an accident. Confined to a wheelchair, he learns to cook and darn, and he becomes a better parent than the obsessive homemaker of a mother—who, in her turn, blossoms from a sour nag into an inspired, joyous, and immensely successful saleswoman. A Jungian would say that, in working out her positive animus creatively, she also freed her husband from the projection of her dissatisfaction. Yet, when he discovers that his injury is psychogenic, he is better able to face a life of deception *in the wheelchair* than society's fundamental contempt for those who work in the home. We cannot, therefore, expect that the eventual self-image of his daughter will be good—if she becomes a wife and mother.

Unlike the 19th century heroine, then, these heroines are portrayed as women who have developed femininity as sexuality (if we mean by this the desire to attract sexually), and even actual responsiveness under certain conditions. These young women seem to have learned to play up to men and to affirm their dominance.[187] Yet as we have seen they do not seem to have developed these abilities through any contact with actual dominant men, fathers or lovers, but rather from the higher authority of advertising, the mass media, and other messages from the public sector.[188]

VI. The Wife in the Mirror: The Husband over Her Shoulder

In a world where being crippled appears to be the best that men can do for their families, a woman's life-problem is no longer how to deserve the title of wife and mother, but rather how to survive it. Hence side by side with the wave of popular books for girls (which were nevertheless equally popular with nostalgic adults), and stories ending in marriage, appear those which either begin with her marriage or launch her rapidly into it, and concern a working out of her identity within or against the context of the marriage. This new formula appears in *Janet Ward* (1902), who, after three chapters of marriage, announces to her husband her intention of taking a trip on her own. Later husbands are not so complaisant.

I have already described the sufferings in *Confessions of a Wife* (1902). Four books that are similar in pattern are *Margaret Warrener* (1901), *The Glass House* (1909), *One Woman's Story* (1916), and *Cecily* (1916). The heroine of each of these stories has a talent or skill, that, unlike Janet, or Harmony of Rinehart's *The Street of Seven Stars* (1914), she is unwilling to relinquish for marital tasks. The woman in *One Woman's Story*, however, modestly calls her musical talent "some outside interest," and the reader is not too surprised to find her husband forbidding her to play the piano in public (even for charity), while he encourages a lovely client to write and publish. *Margaret Warrener*, who relinquished her acting career as a matter of course upon marriage, resigns herself to staying with a husband who no longer loves her, because he is dying of cancer. She supports him, and pays for an operation. ("I'm not worth all this," he justly observes at one point, but he commits suicide rather than give in to his passion for another woman.) The wife in *The Glass House* manages to complete her novel, though her husband "hates the idea" and informs her that if he wins an architectural competition she can "let this novel business go hang." Her book is successful, but she is prostrated. Another heroine, Cecily, (reared by a weakly romantic father and a weakly mercenary mother) learns, during her husband's absence, that she can do without him. They separate, and she supports herself, returning only when she is rescued by him after a traffic accident. "Don't ever go," he begs. "Stay with me always." She does. She even gets pregnant to prove that she will.

While the new ideal of romantic sexuality in marriage meant that women would be encouraged to invest less in their relationship with their children, and more in their attractiveness to their husbands, "typically feminine" selfless or maternal love was hardly discouraged. Yet on the evidence of women's fiction, it appears to have changed in significance. From an illustration of woman's superiority, it has turned into a demonstration of men's inferiority. They need that self-sacrificial, patient support; they are, one knows, "just big little boys."

Of course, a woman can also discover a man is inferior by sheer physical revulsion. While the heroine of domestic sentimental fiction resisted all embraces before marriage, other than the kiss that sealed betrothal, the 20th century heroine often *tests* the quality of a relationship with a kiss, if not a "companionate" marriage.[189] Consequently, there are many discoveries that this man simply will not do. Sometimes, as in *Joretta*, the heroine need not even wash off a drunken kiss to be sure she's made a mistake. She need only look at the man "so big and already inclined to obesity in the revealing bathing suit" to know. Similar ugly revelations occur to the young women in *Secret Marriage, The Lonely Bride, Dawn of the Morning, The State vs. Elinor Norton, Hilltops Clear,* and *Amazing Interlude.* Often, such a discovery is assisted by the occasion of a parallel discovery: There is another man who *will* do. (This does not mean *he* is her superior.)

For example, in *The Mistress of Shenstone,* the heroine is conscious that her marriage to a much older man has left her in a state of "arrested development," but after she had met Jim "a wonderful light dawn[s] in her eyes.... 'Dear God... am I to know the Best?'" Her development, sexually speaking, appears assured. Yet the reader is informed that "the woman's love for the man is essentially unselfish," and poor Myra needs all her unselfishness to cope with this "eternal child—eager, masterful, dependent, full of needs... [so] that, in every woman's love there must... be an element of the eternal mother" This "element" is necessary, even where passionate sexual love is the theme. It is, in fact, the passport to such love.

An example is Rinehart's *Amazing Interlude,* in which the heroine's motherliness, "vicarious, of all the world" prompts her to go to France during World War I to open a soup kitchen. Her rigidly conventional and unimaginative fiancé has failed to "set fire" in her to "the something maternal that is in all women," while "of passion... the terrible love that hurts and agonizes, she had never even dreamed." Over his objections, she goes to France—and to passion, of course. Passion is also the destiny of Robin, of Betty in *The Shuttle,* of the heroine of Hill's novels, and those of Anne Duffield, and of virtually every heroine in fiction after 1925—whether passion *lasts* or not. Yet far more interesting than these displays of romantic dependency is the continuing theme of the emotional endurance of women, compared to men. Women learn again and again, in all sorts of stories, to accept "ordinary"— which appears to mean weak and immature—lovers or husbands. In *Too Young to Marry* (1938), and *A Prince Came Riding* (1940), for example, wives support their husbands. In the latter case, the young woman tells her husband, "Don't ever stop being a glamour boy, Tip darling." In *Heartbroken Melody,* Honor finally feels "sorry" for Paul, "maternal." In *The Lonely Bride* the heroine knows she feels "only tenderness, pity and maternal affection" for her idle husband Roy. In both these cases, a better—though still quite imperfect—man is on the horizon. And the heroines of *Dawn of the Morning, Wife for Sale, Take What You Want,* and *The Hundredth Chance* learn to love (passionately) men they have married for other reasons, a frequent formula in women's fiction, neatly vindicating both marriage and romantic love in the dénouement. In this new fictional formula, then, a young woman transfers her dependency to a man, and a man, moreover, who expects and needs her to act like her mother, while expressing for her in his own inept behavior all her self-doubts about doing anything else. The creation of such new fictional stereotypes suggests that a redefinition rather than a devaluation of mother-hood is in process.

VII. The Wife in the Mirror: The Mother and Children over Her Shoulder

In some earlier stories, hostile or indifferent or even deliberately cruel mothering is depicted: in *The Iron Woman*, *Where the Tide Comes in* ("Mary is always so busy"), *Mara, A Daughter of the Vine* (this mother turns her daughter into an alcoholic like herself: "She put whiskey in my babyfood."), *A Girl of Limberlost*, *Robin* (who is virtually abandoned), *The Homemaker*, *The Promises of Alice* (which were to fulfill *her mother's* missionary ambitions for her), *Janet Ward* (her mother's manic-depressive illness shackles Janet for years), *The Mistress of Shenstone* ("Mamma never allowed her daughters to grow up. We were permitted no individuality of our own."), and *The State vs. Elinor Norton*. And cruel stepmothers still turn up, in *A Bachelor Maid*, *By the Light of the Soul*, and *Her Father's Daughter*. Yet after the 1920s there are hardly any bad mother figures worth remembering in this body of texts. (Of course, many heroines' mothers have died, as is usual in women's fiction. This theme's implications have been fully discussed in earlier chapters.) Mothers in this group of texts are merely drably conventional: Joretta's mother has "dominated and managed her daughter, and the project justified her efforts," while in *Girl in Overalls* "niceness, breeding, what the world thought—meaning what a possible husband thought—those were the impor-tant things" to the heroine's mother. As the heroine says, "I was arguing with Mom . . . but it never gets me anywhere." The post-Freudian generation of popular women writers recognized such maternal attitudes as dangerous, but typically dealt with this problem by ceasing to describe the mothers of central characters much at all. The mothering that these central characters them-selves do is, however, another matter.

As early as *Confessions*, a child's physical health becomes an obviously unhealthy concern. The best-selling novel, *The Awakening of Helena Richie* answers one question: Does she or doesn't she deserve to adopt and raise a little boy? (She does.) In the sequel, *The Iron Woman*, Helena is foil to a mother who has repressed her daughter and spoiled her son. In *The Glass House*, *Cecily*, and *Labyrinth*, the heroine's struggles with husband and career are complicated by guilt over their neglect of their children. In the first of these, the daughter, left unsupervised, is nearly corrupted: "It was my fault—all—all!" her mother cries. In the last, the heroine's mother turns up just long enough to say, helpfully, "I hoped your thinking days were over. Women seem to take pride in being restless, unhappy. We were taught to consider that a sin." When the heroine's little boy has an accident sledding while she is on a business trip, she cannot "even *think* for the present" [emphasis added]. "I've lost my nerve," she tells her employer. "You haven't cared what happened to me," her husband chimes in, and she goes with him when he wants to change his job—leaving hers—because it will be better for the children.

In such a story, if anywhere, we find the real dynamics underlying the "devaluation of motherhood."[190] Especially if she takes seriously the idea that she has other reasons for being, motherhood involves a woman in responsibilities prohibitively complex and confusing. Her confidence that she is naturally suited to the demands and tasks of motherhood, an invaluable comfort to previous busy generations, has been badly eroded, if not destroyed. To be sure, a number of public agencies purportedly stand ready to take over for her, but this is less a consolation than a confirmation of her incapacity. Caught in this dilemma, she is ready to listen to any voice telling her that she can satisfy anyone. So the imperative to give first priority to the needs of others remains.[191] The role of the wife in this body of popular women's fiction appears, in fact, very similar to that of an earlier day, with the important difference that the parent role is reversed: These wives do not neglect ambition, talent, even genius, because a paternal husband ordered them to do so. They do it because these boys they've picked *demand mothering*; this value, as much as the one of sexual attractiveness, constrains the women's roles depicted. "I'll never let you go," the heroine assures her husband in *Wife for Sale* (1934) "in her tender young motherly voice," and "the smile Barry gave her she thought might be the same smile a lonely little affectionate [boy] had given his invalid mother years ago."

VIII. The Wife in the Mirror: How Old Is She?

This matter-of-fact assumption of a supportive role would seem incompatible with the new concern for the attractions of youthfulness in the heroine; in fact, the two are regularly portrayed as one quality. Where aging is depicted with real pathos or even horror, it is *Mother's* aging (in *Janet Ward, Robin, The Shuttle*—where, however, a woman is rejuvenated by her young, supportive sister—or in *Stella Dallas*). More frequently, youthfulness is part of the quality that enables daughters to accomplish what their (weak or timid or trapped) mothers could not: the extra-domestic, if modest, successes of *Hilltops Clear*, of most of Hill's and Norris's heroines, of Sidney in *K.*, Elnora in *A Girl of the Limberlost*, Wilkins/Freeman's heroines, Banning's, Duffield's, Doran's, and Grey's. Working girls all, their youth is in no way a disadvantage to them. It means vitality and enthusiasm just as it means sexual desirability.

In longer and more complex fictions, such as Parrish's *To-morrow Morning* (1927), Barnes's *Years of Grace* (1931), and Winsor's *Star Money* (1950), the signs of physical aging accompany the waning of a neglected talent. The heroine of *To-morrow Morning* will never resume her painting career, and complains, "Look at my hands and my scrawny old neck," to herself in the mirror. "I feel old," says the heroine of *Star Money* to her lover, who could "tell her she was not actually beautiful and reduce her to cringing abject submission" (although *she* is supporting him) "for her face, after all, was the reflection of her self."

Yet this emphasis on youthfulness, I am suggesting, stems in part from a source other than a male-dominated economic structure that tended to overvalue desirable female bodies. A woman's strength of purpose, her very autonomy, is identified in book after book with youthfulness, in a way that goes well beyond any realistic assessment of the waning of adolescent idealism, high spirits, or even physical well-being.[192] Heroines are women who try not to repeat their mothers' lives, who at least for a time break from their pattern, who do *better* than their mothers in any of several acceptable ways. They get an education, make a career, and make (especially in pre-1929 stories) a "good" marriage. This betterment is the new imperative, and the ambiguities inherent in the role of Daughter of the Future are at least as taxing as those in 19th century roles for women. "The vision of the future as the commodity market dangled before women's eyes," comments Ewen, was of "a society in which . . . women might expect their daughters' lives to transcend the historic limitations of their own."[193] Mothers in these books are shown sacrificing their happiness for their daughters' happiness while daughters scarcely ever sacrifice anything for their mothers anymore. *Stella Dallas* is the most stunning example, but others occur in books of the early decades of the century, and throughout Norris's and Hill's work. As early as 1911, the daughter in *Mother* says, "You owe your husband something, you owe yourself something. I want to get on, to study and travel, to be a companion to my husband," and in Miller's *Come Out of the Kitchen* (1916) a girl "imagined that she had thoroughly emancipated herself from her mother's dominance because she had established a different field of interest [than] domestic management." More and more frequently after the early 1920s Mother merely provides a full background for the brilliant, strong, competent daughter.

"Scorn in the adult . . . reveals personal uncertainty about one's self-worth," Chasseguet-Smirguel wrote in 1976. "My experience has shown me that underlying this scorn one always finds a powerful maternal image, envied and terrifying."[194] She is writing of men, but the words are immensely suggestive as well of the sort of heroines I have been describing, not least in their attempt to be male-identified. A 1937 heroine tells herself desperately that "she had to prove to herself that she had iron and stamina—guts!" (*Pay* for Your Pleasure), while scorning men and mother together. As Horney put it, girls who think there is something wrong with them take refuge "in a fictitious male role." The "bravado" which a family doctor identifies in the heroine of Girl in Overalls is as much a revolt against her mother's demands as it is a protection against men. She fears both, and the object of the fear may be one.

Women, told by their rapidly changing culture that they can and should enjoy such previously male prerogatives as independent careers (with all the rationality, competence, and focussed, unflagging energy this implies) and passionate sexuality as well, are not surprisingly terrified and envious of even the "good" aspect of the maternal image, threatening to trap them into imitation. Nor is it any wonder that terror and envy of the men who replace Mother in their lives result in persistently devaluating fantasies of them, as well.

In a discussion of what he terms the second individuation phase of adolescence, Peter Blos speaks of a "frantic turn to reality."[195] The term reality is defined for the psychoanalyst by its opposition to the term fantasy, but for my purposes it needs some further explanation. "Dream and reality became equated in the world of ideas generated by the marketplace,"[196] comments Ewen, in his book on the growth of the consumer culture and its collective dreams of the desirable. Work, illness, war, travel, lodging, day-to-day necessity, or accomplishment—all of these, in the early 20th century, begin to be defined by the mass products which are advertised as essential embellishments or symbols of such experiences or, if an experience is a problem, as a solution to it. When the heroines of these stories succeed in dealing with "real" issues, then, it is only through the mediation of objects which they are taught to use by the laws of this collective dreamworld.[197] Not least among such objects are those that promise to keep them looking young.

IX. The Wife in the Mirror: Where in the World Can She Go?

Most of these heroines fulfill the American social imperative to be "better" than their parents, and are portrayed as acquiring a social and economic status superior to that of their mothers. The imperative is a psychological one also. In the sort of narcissistic personality I have been describing, the superego's values (because they are still those of the harsh pre-oedipal superego) are experienced as absolute. In such personalities we can expect ambition of a particularly anxious sort, needing a great deal of obvious reassurance: a denial of normal dependency, but overdependency on external signs of esteem or worth.[198] In story after story, the feminine version of Horatio Alger's culture myth is enacted, as a poor (but well-bred) girl marries a rich man.

In other stories, material success, usually of a modest sort, is achieved through the young woman's own efforts. However, her working hours are seldom, if ever, described in any detail. With one exception, it is the result, not the fact or process of work, that is emphasized. Deland's *Iron Woman*, and Stratton-Porter's girls who hunt wild asparagus and butterflies are exceptions, as is Canfield/Fisher's saleswoman. Nursing (as in the case of Sidney, in *K.*), teaching, and writing are accorded slightly less description than they were in the domestic fiction of the 19th century. In *Girl in Overalls*, we hear something about operations in the airplane factory where the heroine, Rusty, works, but not about *her* work. No other women's jobs are more than mentioned. This in itself might suggest nothing in particular: a faithful account of secretarial work, for example, would be unlikely to add to the popular appeal of a romantic book, and where a serious treatment of an artistic career is attempted it takes the book out of that category. (For example, Cather's *Song of the Lark*, and Davenport's *Of Lena Geyer*, belong to this period: They are not romantic fiction.) The fact that makes such an omission seem sinister is this: *Housework*, despite its claims to be as boring as the assembly line, is repeatedly given long, fascinated, and detailed description, surpassing even those of the whole new wardrobe. From Wilkins/Freeman's books, in which darning, ironing, dusting, cooking, and furnishing a house occupy pages, to Winsor's lengthy description of the appointments of her star's urban apartment, keeping house is regularly included.

Several reasons for this come to mind. The 19th century sexual division of labor took place in a world that increasingly seemed to threaten "home," as a way of giving it value. Perhaps this mechanism is being cranked up again, under the influx of corporate goods and state expertise, and what little productive value still clings to home is being emphasized in reaction to this danger of invasion. These fictional celebrations may, then, be attempts to hold on to a vanishing ideal by those writing (in important part) for housewives. However, this overevaluation of houses and housekeeping has other causes.

It has already been suggested that a woman's house may be symbolic of her self, or of her mother, or even both simultaneously. This identification alone, especially in a narcissistic personality, could create the perfectionism depicted in these books. In *The Homemaker*, Eva, who spends the first two pages of the novel scrubbing the kitchen floor, is by page 268 "a splendid woman . . . a stylish-looking woman. There wasn't anybody in town could hold a candle to her." She has now become one of the fortunate few who need not displace the new concern with physical attractiveness to her house. Over and above such an interpretation, however, there is much that is worth examining in the way the subject of housekeeping is dealt with in this body of fiction.

In *Janet Ward* (1902), we are not surprised to hear two older women call a younger one "the saving salt of our society. The homekeeping, homemaking conservative woman"—but it comes as a shock when a young woman portrayed throughout as talented, large-souled, independent, and ambitious ends up "taking orders for pictures and something still more interesting, the decoration and proper furnishing of artistic homes." Stratton-Porter (*Her Father's Daughter*, 1921) has a brilliant woman succeed in an architectural competition because of her original design for the kitchen in her house. (This prematurely white-haired young woman, by the way, drove the car in the accident that was fatal to her parents—and the heroine's as well. So perhaps she can be seen as having special needs for acts of reparation.) Sidney, in *K.* "had been born in the little brick house, and, as she was of it, so it was of her. Her hands had smoothed and painted the pine floors [and] . . . with what agonies of slacking lime and adding blueing, whitewashed the fence itself!" When Harmony, in *The Street of Seven Stars*, has decided she can no longer live with her beloved doctor and his patient, she leaves the rooms "warm and cheery," the table set, dinner ready. The message in all such stories is clear: It does not matter what else you do well; you must keep house well. A career which allows you to do *both* is of course best.

Grace Livingston Hill's heroines, from 1910 on, find that they have to make a home for themselves, and their careful ingenuity is meticulously described. "There was a hardware store next door, and here she found a partial solution to her fire problem in canned alcohol and a little outfit for cooking with it. She also invested in some paper plates and cups, a sharp knife, a pair of good scissors, a hammer, a can opener, some tacks, and a few long nails" (*Not Under the Law*). Joyce is furnishing a cottage which would have been a wreck had she not persuaded the workmen to move it for her—the vine covering it intact. She is also portrayed as saving another woman from domestic disaster: Having burned the chops for a company dinner, she must be taught a new way to prepare ham. A great deal of *Crimson Roses* is given over to Marion's search for lodging (after her brother has deceived her and sold the family home her father meant her to have). She makes do, much as Joyce does, but is rewarded for her efforts. After her marriage she "entered the great, handsome house, and looked about upon the beauty and luxury which were henceforth to be hers." The girl in *Ladybird* is forced to make her home for a night in a tree, where she dreams "if only Mother were back, and they two could have a home of their own, where joy and safety and love abode!" She takes a job as a social secretary, but is unsatisfied: The work "seemed so indefinite and desultory . . . . It seemed to her that she was not giving enough service for all she was receiving," and she ultimately leaves the position for a fourth floor room with a tiny grimy window and a job pulling bastings in a sweatshop.

Other heroines, until they are safely married, must create homes for themselves, and sometimes for their brothers and sisters, under difficult circumstances. In Norris's *Secret Marriage* and *Wife for Sale*, there are quite explicit descriptions of just how to do this. In *Wife for Sale*, after several pages detailing the sordid petty bleakness of urban homemaking (canned piecrust is mentioned with particular horror), Norah arranges, by a marriage of convenience, to transport her family to a country house. Page after page describes the refurbishing and refurnishing of the house, as well as how they manage to eat. At one point Norah falls asleep redecorating the parlor. In *Secret Marriage*, Mary must give up her childhood home. "A spasm of love for her home came over Mary and made her feel faint for a moment.... Oh, they couldn't live anywhere else!" She and her brothers and sisters move, however, to a small house in "a dreary state of ruin"—pages describe the dirt, rubbish, and grease she can never quite clean out. Yet this house, which she can *work on*, she prefers to the home in which her husband wants her to take her place: "a doll's house . . . putting her back in childhood." Of course the camping-out quality of the arrangements these girls contrive on their own will have already suggested childhood games to the reader. Prue, in Loring's *Hilltops Clear*, is described as having a repapering complex, and when she and her brother have to remove to the country she transfers her "craft of designer and maker of jewelry" to the house and farm, arranging books, flowers, vegetable garden, fencing the poultry yard, and—of course—repainting and papering the house.

The amount of effort expended itself appears to confer value on domestic work. Even the wealthy Joretta, reduced—by an elopement—to keeping house in a "tawdry and garish" apartment, is inspired to a three-page struggle with a washing machine and clothesline—while the beans scorch. And when her domineering mother's illness takes her home, she now feels a guest in a strange house where there is *nothing to do*. The heroine of *Woman with a Past* tells (for two pages) how she has redecorated a house so that no vestige of the past remains: "'I was half-crazy. I think the house shows it.' Amelia said hopefully."

Meals are provided for men with stunning regularity in love stories of the 1930s and 1940s, always proving the fundamental womanliness of the cook, and always receiving masculine approval. In *His Secretary*, for example, the boss gets roast beef, broccoli with Hollandaise sauce, a green salad, and lemon pie. The emphasis on pleasing men in this fashion seems the obvious result of the dictates of the mass media after the first World War.[199] Yet it is equally clear that the "perfect" wife–companion portrayed in this period, "creating" home and nourishment with such passion, is doing more than fulfilling an image from women's magazines.

The returns to mother–child symbiosis enacted in these fictional marriages, though they sound so final when entered into, are nevertheless fantasies that need bolstering up daily by all the nurturant activity at the fantasists' command. And even then it doesn't always work: "I sometimes feel as if these walls were just waiting to see something happen," a married daughter complains to her mother in Barnes's 1831 best-seller *Years of Grace*, "Something *ought* to happen in a room as charming as this. I feel just that way about everything, Mumsy—about my clothes and the way I look and all the trouble I take about the maids and the meals and the children; I'm everlastingly setting the stage . . . . Oh, I don't know what I want! Just girlhood over again, I guess." In this novel, the daughter goes off with another man; her mother's decision not to so do has been the subject of the first half of the book. Of course this final act of denial and independence is only the usual substitution of a new symbiosis for an old one.

The fictional invention of practical and social difficulties for the heroine to overcome in getting "home" at last, the unmistakable tone of bliss with which beautiful homes where a symbiotic arrangement is working are described, indicate almost as great a degree of emotional involvement as we saw in the last chapter. The emphasis, however, seems to have shifted from a replication of Mother's home, a more or less uninterrupted search for a place in which to be just like her, to acts of rather irrelevant reparation for the guilt of being as *unlike* her as possible. These new heroines are depicted as having betrayed their mothers by elopements, careers, actual sexual misdemeanors, changes of social class, and simple disloyalty to home values. All the more reason, apparently, to scrupulously decorate, maintain, and ceremonialize the home and its remaining functions.[200] To repeat Von Franz's description: "When she is alone her animus assures her that she is lonely and nobody and nothing and will never get anywhere." So she gets busy on details. (In Burnett's *The Shuttle* [1907] the plot turns on getting the hero to accept the heroine's money in order to restore his huge old estate.)

The obsession with domestic detail, as we have seen, is intensified by conflicts between the role of housekeeper and career woman or artist. Guilt and anxiety seem to increase in proportion to the character's achievements outside the traditional sphere. "I can't do it," Catherine in *Labyrinth* thinks. "Too many things. *Things!* That's it. Clothes, and laundry, and dirt in the corners." And later, after she has been working outside the home, "There's not a bill that isn't larger, in spite of everything that I can do. Food, laundry, clothes. You have no idea how much I was worth! As a labor device, I mean." She is portrayed as imprisoned in routine details, in the fashion characteristic of the animus-possessed—but *in the home*; her work (which we hear little about) seems to be going smoothly. In *To-morrow Morning*, with greater pathos, the central character paints the kitchen "bright blue, with white woodwork. And there were little things to do—the plants to be watered, an angel cake to make for the Altar Guild party, a dress to smock—It was always nearly lunch time when she was ready to begin work in the studio, and it seemed inappropriate to recommence a career at a quarter past twelve. Better wait until the next morning and start right."

In 1929, a contemporary observer could already remark of the "things" that plagued women like those in these stories, that "as the demand for luxuries, artificially stimulated by advertising, mounts giddily higher there is no help for it—the women have to go to work.... But... women have inherited the home as their job; there is no evidence that the wage-earning woman will try to evade the job that she accepted at mother's knee." Mother's knee, or husband's? It hardly seems to matter. "Between [the housewife] and the world of reality stands the figure of her husband; from him she derives her major satisfactions, to him she attributes the causes of her major discontents."[201] One of the major discontents which a wife in this book projects onto her husband in the "world of reality" is an affair with an independent careerwoman.

X. The Shadow in the Mirror: She Goes to Work

The American woman of the first four decades of this century was to be meticulous housewife, intelligent and informed and loving mother to children (and husband), sexually desirable and responsive to her husband, better than her mother in every way, and fashionably attractive. The figure of an independent and selfish career woman is "cast into the shadow" in all these romances, undoubtedly, because this unrealized potential in women is so threatening to all the other roles and—as such—an unrealized desire as well. These narcissistic heroines separate their love and hate; their hidden rage surfaces powerfully in what these shadow characters get away with.[202] (They do not, of course, get away with it to the end of these stories.)

As early as Margaret Warrener, One Woman's Story, and A Bachelor Maid, the shadow figure is a woman with a career. In Labyrinth we meet another, who tells the wife, Catherine, (not yet working herself) "I'm not a bit domestic," and impresses the husband with her serenity and charm while Catherine serves dinner, puts children to bed, and cleans up. The physical attractiveness of all these working women is emphasized; indeed the category overlaps with another—that of the frivolously, superficially independent society woman, who appears in, for example, Hill's books, as well as A Girl of the Limberlost, Secret Marriage, Robin, Daughter of the Vine, and You Can't Escape, where the heroine looks "like a child" beside the blatant sexual charms of the shadow figure—who is doing very well at running "a little dress shop." The heroine is explicitly admired by the hero as "a girl who isn't running around after a career."

In Chapter Three I described how, toward the end of the 19th century, a new character type, the redeemed shadow, began to appear. This other sort of shadow figure occurs frequently in the fiction of the early decades of this century. There is Helena Richie, who repents her adultery, and Elizabeth, in the sequel, *The Iron Woman*, who must learn to control her passionate nature. There is the alcoholic Daughter of the Vine and the secretly married heroine of *A Far Away Princess*, who travels incognito, is a French actress, deceives her husband's family—but is finally reconciled with them. There is the heroine of *The Heart's Kingdom*, who has been raised by a father who is an atheist and a drunkard, and redeems her cynicism and callousness by seeing that her fiancé makes an honest woman of a girl he has wronged. In Ethel M. Dell's 1917 best-seller *The Hundredth Chance*, the heroine redeems her love for the man not her husband, by finally falling in love with her husband, going into a burning stable to save his prize racehorse, and then buying him the Stud he has always wanted! There are passionate and silly girls in Stratton-Porter's novels, who learn better, either by bitter experience (Eileen, comments the heroine of *Her Father's Daughter*, "had been redeemed . . . a new heart and a new soul . . . even . . . a new body. Her face is not the same." Eileen's experience has been living with gross and tasteless rich relatives), or by the example of the heroine, as in *A Girl of the Limberlost*, where a society girl finally tells her fiancé, "I'll be the other kind of a girl, as fast as I can learn." Similarly the shadow figure of *You Can't Escape* envies the heroine as having "no conception of what loving could mean, claws in your breast, tearing, bloody, terrible . . . pitiless and compulsory." She subsequently watches the patient suffering of the heroine, and learns to want to be like her. By attending a petting party, the frivolous and flippant Charlotte so enrages her sister Rusty in *Girl in Overalls* that Rusty nearly strangles her. Later she tells Rusty "I needed killing . . . you're getting grander all the time," and takes her advice on dating practices. There are the heroines of Norris's *Mother*, and *Heartbroken Melody*, who are seduced by jobs promising riches and social prestige into a betrayal of home values, and learn better. Honor's penance is the hardest: She loses health and beauty. Margaret merely has a revelation concerning her sister Julie, who "had forgotten Europe, forgotten all the ideal ambitions of her girlhood because she loved her husband . . . ." Of her own fiancé, Margaret dreams: "to be shut away with him from all the world but the world of their own four walls—why that would be the greatest happiness of all!"

Clearly these headlong plunges into symbiotic domesticity do not represent the attainment or integration of a mature sexuality. What *do* they represent? It is the position of many feminist historians that as American consumerism took hold, women began to be stupified by the desire for the pleasures that the country's new affluence, and the doubled volume of advertising, promised them. Sometime in the 1920s they began to give up seriousness of purpose, in order to be the "kept" wives of urban businessmen and, later, corporation men commuting to suburbia.[203] There is another aspect to the new overinvestment in family life which began to take place in this period. Throughout this century, many observers believe, the family has been reorganized into a mechanism of social control by the purchase of authority itself, in such forms as doctors or good schools. Through a series of interventions by these agents and bureaucracies, the family is encouraged to renounce "the question of political right, through the private pursuit of well-being."[204] American women, in particular, have allied themselves with these new forces of socialization, because of the American woman's traditional role as culture-bearer, and traditional desire for betterment. Neither aspect of consumer culture encourages adult autonomy *or* relationship.

XI. Going Home Again

Are these women qualitatively different from the examples of "true womanhood" portrayed in the preceding chapter? Do they bypass the acts of sacrifice, renunciation, and reparation which characterized good and redeemed women of the earlier fictional period? We have seen that the fictional evidence of the 1920s and the following decades does not indicate that this wholesale reversal of values in fact takes place. The same need to make up to mother for going beyond her merely emerges in different forms. The 1923 story of *Stella Dallas* is one example: Laurel will never, we know, have to work or sacrifice a day in her life. Yet the story itself is an embodiment of the need for reparation: a glorification of the self-sacrificing mother in the very act of rejecting her. In the 1930s and 1940s, the Daughters of the Future begin to produce themselves, and fictional mothers, as I have commented, either disappear or appear somehow neutralized. Now the problem seems to center around sexual relationships. (The two problems are of course still closely related.)

"American women of the twenties," Sochen comments, "accepted their sex-determined roles, and did not want to risk . . . the loss of love."[205] As Banner puts it, writing of the 1930s, "in this time of economic security, the family assumed a new importance in the social structure: the home was, after all, one place where the individual could find emotional sustenance . . . . Partly people were staying home and staying married because they could not afford to do otherwise."[206]

When women were encouraged to return from the labor market to the home in the 1930s,[207] the old-fashioned split in real-life and fictional roles persisted. However, during the 1940s the call went out for women, including married women in new numbers, to engage in nontraditional jobs outside the home, and they responded.[208] This time, when the war ended, they did not go home again. At the same time, women's fiction responded to the changed climate of opinion. In the 1940s the historical romance appeared, with a central character who is herself an irredeemably ambitious woman, such as Scarlett O'Hara, du Maurier's Rebecca, or Winsor's Amber. These fictional women may fall in love, but they remain manipulative, self-centered in the extreme, and sometimes even sexually "liberated," on the masculine model. A good woman appears—but *overshadowed* by this central character. Romantic fiction set in the present during the 1940s specializes in movie stars (for example, in *Together*, and *Suddenly It's Love*) who need to be selfish to get to the top; by the 1950s this shadow figure will blend the two tendencies, toward personal ambition and an overt and often amoral sexual competitiveness with all other women. The dominant culture also responded to the war by emphasizing woman's domestic and feminine roles with increasing fervor.[209] In terms of attitudes, Sochen claims, the decades of the 1940s and the 1950s were "of one piece."[210] At the end of the 1943 story *Girl in Overalls*, the heroine a bit prematurely promises her fiancé to quit work as soon as the war is over, and tells him "women couldn't change."

By the end of the 1920s, as we have seen, "love," whatever the underlying psychodynamic, was defined as romantic and sexual. The premise was that this pleasure was yet another new source of domestic enjoyment, like the radio and electric kitchen ranges. Add such a belief to the almost undiminished social value of wifehood, and the new cultural imperative to be good in the marriage bed is strong indeed. It has been strengthened in the 20th century by more than the messages of the mass media, however. As long as women idealized their mothers, they could also idealize themselves, good object and good self-representations combining to provide at least a workable illusion of ego strength. This illusion was the source of the moral certainty, the sometimes smug self-satisfaction, shown by Hentz's or Evans's heroines as they played out their prescribed 19th century dramas. It is most definitely a thing of the past for the heroines of this chapter, in which mothers have ceased to be useful role models. The psychological picture is different, as well. Mothers, even when strong, are not idealized. The most powerful psychic representation of a mother, on the evidence of this fiction, is bad, and moreover receives the projection of the child's own rage. The stage of psychological development I am describing is beyond symbiosis, and provides ego boundaries. Yet because the loss of the idealized image of other and self is *not* complemented by a loss of the fantasized *bad* images of other and self, nor the harsh superego which accompanies them, ego strength is lost. Women are shown as having gained in the ability to face reality, both internal and external, but they are not shown as able to enjoy this gain. The depressive position, while a stage of development beyond symbiosis, is painful and—particularly—lonely.[211] To its burdens these heroines add the burdens of narcissistic, anxious ambition. If this stage is not a precursor to integration, regression is likely to follow.

Imagine then a cohort of young women experiencing the loneliness of this new inner emptiness, and strong demands by the super-ego. In the late 1920s, and the decades that followed, a whole new body of fiction sprang into being, and its heroines are without exception lonely overachievers, as anxious in their own spheres as the desperate housekeepers I have already discussed. Arcadia House, Godwin Publishers, Phoenix Press, A.L. Burt, Grosset and Dunlap, Penn and Gramercy Publishing Companies, Triangle Press, and others turned out by hundreds inexpensive hardcover books bearing such titles as *The Petter*, *When a Girl Loves*, *Repent at Leisure*, *Halfway to Paradise*, *Brief Rapture*, *Hometown Angel*, *If I Loved You Less*, *His Own Wife* and (by the same writer) *A Husband to Keep*, *Six Times a Bride*, *Careless Caresses*, *Girl Next Door* and (by the same writer) *Love Slave*. Written by women with as many as half-a-dozen pen names, these series of "love" stories illustrate themes long popular in the sensation novel, and sensational new topics, such as abortion, as well as the themes and topics which have defined the women's fiction I have been describing in this study. Though most of these writers were well into middle age or beyond it, they shared an ability to redeem their central characters from situations which would have been considered impossible before World War I. These fictional young women have had several lovers (*Pay for Your Pleasure*), have done time in prison (*Woman with a Past*), associated with members of the underworld (*Tabloid Love*, *His Secretary*)—or, in some stories, they have merely fallen in love with a brother-in-law, their married employer, or out of love with a husband.

By the 1930s, one scholar of best-sellers believes, plots turning on problems of pre- or extramarital sex, or divorce, had lost some of their excitement. She feels that the new tone indicates that unfaithfulness lost its status as rebellion, and became just another "part of family relations."[212] It is true that the popular series Loring and Duffield are still selling portray sexual irregularities in a manner both perfunctory and drab. The explanation for this emotional impoverishment (portending the "zombie" condition of the 1950s and 1960s heroines is probably not so simple. Strong feelings these new heroines do have—but they appear to alternate between loneliness (often described as a sense of emptiness; one heroine feels "hollow and uninhabited"—*You Can't Escape*) and bliss at the relief of loneliness.

"My wife," breathes the hero of *So Deep My Love*. "Dee liked the sound of the word, the possessiveness of it, the belonging. It was like a promise she would never be alone again." In *Together*, the lonely heroine, maintaining her typical bravado, broods "if Jim knew that behind her show of indifference she was weak and vulnerable . . . he would despise her . . . . The temptation to pour out all her loneliness and secret fears terrified her," and when he calls her "baby," she becomes hysterical. She needs a lot of soothing before she can give up her defenses, which include an interest in business and wearing slacks. In each of these novels, despite some apparent confusion, only *one* man can rescue the girl from "bitterness and disillusionment . . . make her face the question: Had she a soul worth regenerating?" (from the front-piece synopsis to *Pay for Your Pleasure*). Unfeminine, immoral, criminal behavior, all can finally be swept away as if they had never been, by the girl's tenacious hold onto one love object: "since that night," Amelia claims (one marriage and two lovers later), "I have never loved anyone but you" (*Woman with a Past*). A similar emotional fidelity often characterizes the otherwise promiscuous heroines of historical romances. And at the end of *Tabloid Love*, the heroine, who had once decided, "cold-bloodedly," not to surrender to marriage, who had purposely "armored herself" against it, actually requests a spanking from her future husband on the book's last page. Clearly infidelity lacks the excitement of rebellion because it is no rebellion, but rather a search for security. In a mechanism which is by now familiar, the more frantically—even luridly—dependency is denied, the more thoroughly it is yielded to at last, so these fictional women can accept their place, in a man's arms.

Also, in the 1930s, such writers as Stonebraker, Grey, and Duffield begin to write tamer stories, about the sort of heroine popularized in the fiction of Norris, Loring, and Baldwin, whose behavior is far less rash, but quite as self-defeating; their inheritors are the writers of the Harlequin Romance popular today. "In that warm circle of his arms she was sheltered and at peace," a Loring heroine claims in 1970 (*No Time for Love*).

This collection of heroines, as we have seen, do not suffer from the need to replicate one image, and that, mother's, like the 19th century heroine. Their problem is rather that of needing to reflect too many images, play too many roles: mother, yes, but also domestic scientist, lover, woman of the world, careerist. Their world is a world of mirrors in which they search endlessly—always frustrated—for a self they can admire. Others are mirrors for them; they themselves are only real in these mirrors, most especially in the eyes of the men they eventually stop the search to marry. Their empty inner world demands too much of them; their outer world promises too much fulfillment, and encourages them to measure themselves by personal and material standards. No wonder they stop polishing mirrors to fall into the "mirror stare," and stop staring to fall into a husband's arms.

The period in women's fiction between 1880 and 1950 was clearly one of dis-integration. But in the 1950s, while fictional heroines still failed at the task of integration, they began to do so in a new coherent, popular genre, that of romantic suspense fiction or the "new gothic." The next chapter will deal with this anomaly.

The Texts

Page numbers of important references to these texts, as they appear in sequence in this chapter, follow each bibliographical citation.

Alden, Isabella ("Pansy"). *Mara*. Boston: Lothrup Publishing Co., 1903.

Ashley, Ellen. *Girl in Overalls*. New York: Dodd, Mead and Co., 1943. (1–2, 266)

Atherton, Gertrude. *Black Oxen*. New York: Boni and Liveright, 1923.

———. *A Daughter of the Vine.* New York: John Lane, 1899. (188)

Bailey, Temple. *Silver Slippers*. Philadelphia: Pennsylvania Pub. Co., 1928. (85, 21)

Baldwin, Faith. *Take What You Want*. New York: Holt, Rinehart and Winston, 1970.

———. *White Collar Girl*. New York: Farrar and Rinehart, 1933.

———. *You Can't Escape*. New York: Aeonian Press, 1943. (121, 27–28)

Banning, Margaret Culkin. *Too Young To Marry*. New York: Harper and Brothers, 1938.

Barclay, Florence L. *The Mistress of Shenstone*. New York: Grosset and Dunlap, 1910. (16, 253, 335, 32)

———. *The Rosary*. New York: G.P. Putnam's Sons, 1909. (266)

Barnes, Margaret Ayer. *Years of Grace*. New York: Houghton Mifflin, 1931. (470–471)

Beecher, Carolyn. *One Woman's Story*. New York: Britton Pub. Co., 1919. (85)

Brener, Marguerite. *Empty Arms*. New York: The Macaulay Co., 1935. (9)

Brown, Alice. *Margeret Warrener*. Boston: Houghton, Mifflin and Co., 1901. (388)

Brucker, Margaretta. *His Secretary*. New York: Gramercy Pub. Co., 1944.

———. *Together*. New York: Arcadia House, 1945. (14, 67, 149)

Bryan, Mary E. *Ruth, the Outcast*. New York: George Munro, 1887.

Burnett, Frances Hodgson. *Robin*. New York: Frederick A. Stokes Co., 1922.

———. *The Shuttle*. New York: Frederick A. Stokes Co., 1907. (223)

Canfield/Fisher, Dorothy. *The Homemaker*. New York: Harcourt, Brace and Co., 1924.

Clay, Bertha M. *Violet Lisle*. New York: Street and Smith, 1892. (13)

Corbett, Elizabeth. *Cecily and the Wide World*. New York: Henry Holt and Co., 1916. (331–337)

Daviess, Maria. *The Heart's Kingdom*. Chicago: Reilly and Britton Co., 1917.

Deland, Margaret. *The Awakening of Helena Richie*. New York: Harper and Brothers, 1905.

———. *The Iron Woman*. New York: Harper and Brothers, 1911.

———. *The Promises of Alice*. New York: Harper and Brothers, 1919.

Dell, Ethel M. *The Bars of Iron*. New York: G.P. Putnam's Sons, 1916.

———. *The Hundredth Chance*. New York: G.P. Putnam's Sons, 1917.

Doran, Janet. *The Prince Came Riding*. New York: Gramercy Pub. Co., 1940.

Duffield, Anne. *The Lonely Bride*. New York: Arcadia House, 1947.

———. *Repent at Leisure*. New York: Arcadia House, 1946.

Gaddis, Peggy. *Suddenly It's Love*. New York: Arcadia House, 1949.

Grey, Viven. *Let's Call It Love*. New York: Arcadia House, 1948.

————. *So Deep My Love*. New York: Arcadia House, 1944. (24)

Harrison, Constance. *A Bachelor Maid*. New York: The Century Co., 1894. (31, 16–17, 145)

Hill, Grace Livingston. *According to the Pattern*. Philadelphia: Griffith and Rowland Press, 1903.

————. *Crimson Roses*. New York: J.B. Lippincott, 1928. (267, 283, 319)

————. *Dawn of the Morning*. New York: J.B. Lippincott, 1911. (reissued in Bantam edition, 1975)

————. *Ladybird*. New York: J.B. Lippincott, 1930. (Reissued in Bantam edition, 1979) (86, 177)

————. *Not Under the Law*. New York: J.B. Lippincott, 1925. (142)

Hull, Helen R. *Labyrinth*. New York: The Macmillan Co., 1923. (58, 294, 324, 332–334, 36, 148)

Hurst, Vida. *Pretty Polly*. New York: Gramercy Pub. Co., 1943.

Kingsley, Florence. *The Glass House*. New York: Dodd, Mead and Co., 1909. (99, 191, 58)

Lee, Patricia. *Tabloid Love*. New York: Godwin Publishers, 1936.

Libbey, Laura Jean. *The Clutch of the Marriage Tie: A Story of the Second Class*. Brooklyn: Publisher's Printing Co., 1920.

Loring, Emilie. *Hilltops Clear*. New York: Grosset and Dunlap, 1933.

————. *No Time for Love*. Boston: Little, Brown and Co., 1970. (280)

Miller, Alice Duer. *Come Out of the Kitchen! A Romance*. New York: Grosset and Dunlap, 1916. (922)

Norris, Kathleen. *Heartbroken Melody*. New York: Doubleday Doran and Co., 1938. (21, 39, 89, 167)

————. *Home*. New York: E.P. Dutton and Co., 1928.

————. *Mother*. New York: The Macmillan Co., 1912. (9, 160–161)

————. *Secret Marriage*. Garden City: Doubleday Doran and Co., 1936. (43–44, 212)

————. *Wife for Sale*. Garden City: Doubleday Doran and Co., 1935. (355–336)

Parrish, Anne. *To-morrow Morning*. New York: Harper and Brothers, 1927. (13, 162, 175, 274)

Prouty, Olive Higgins. *Stella Dallas*. New York: Houghton Mifflin and Co., 1923. (303)

Rinehart, Mary Roberts. *Amazing Interlude*. New York: Grosset and Dunlap, 1918. (23, 29, 24)

————. *K*. New York: Grosset and Dunlap, 1915. (11)

————. *The State vs. Elinor Norton*. New York: P.F. Collier, 1934.

————. *The Street of Seven Stars*. New York: Grosset and Dunlap, 1914. (164)

Sangster, Margaret E. *Janet Ward: A Daughter of the Manse*. New York: Fleming H. Revall Co., 1902. (77, 14, 94–95, 178)

Slottman, Leona (as Gladys Stone). *Three Nights of Love.* New York: Phoenix Press, 1946.

———— (as Carlotta Baker). *Woman with a Past.* New York: Phoenix Press, 1940. (249)

Stonebraker, Florence (as Florenz Branch). *Pay for Your Pleasure.* New York: Phoenix Press, 1937. (131)

———— (as Florence Stuart). *The Shelf Full of Dreams.* New York: Arcadia House, 1949. (252)

Stratton-Porter, Gene. *A Girl of the Limberlost.* New York: Doubleday, Page, and Co., 1910. (481)

————. *Her Father's Daughter.* Garden City: The Country Life Press, 1921. (3, 475)

Thruston, Lucy Meacham. *Where the Tide Comes In.* Boston: Little, Brown and Co., 1904. (49)

Tiernan, Frances (as Christian Reid). *A Far Away Princess.* New York: Devin-Adair Co., 1914.

Ward, Elizabeth Stuart Phelps (as Mary Adams). *Confessions of a Wife.* New York: The Century Co., 1902. (104)

Webster, Edna Robb. *Joretta.* New York: Grosset and Dunlap, 1932. (90, 3)

Wiggin, Kate Douglas. *Rose O' the River.* New York: The Century Co., 1905.

Wilcox, Ella Wheeler. *Sweet Danger.* Chicago: M.A. Donahue, 1902.

Wilkins/Freeman, Mary E. *By the Light of the Soul.* New York: Harper and Brothers, 1907. (4, 153)

————. *Pembroke.* New York: Harper and Brothers, 1894.

————. *The Portion of Labor.* New York: Harper and Brothers, 1901. (133-134)

Winsor, Kathleen. *Star Money.* New York: Appleton Century Crofts, 1950. (123, 382)

5

THE DREAM OF SPACE:
Romantic Suspense Fiction Since 1950

I. Suburban Spaces and the New Genre

The rise of the genre of the "new gothic" follows a change in American demography almost as important from our point of view as the shift from a predominantly rural to a predominantly urban population. In the late 1940s, the move to the suburbs began: Between 1950 and 1960 nearly two-thirds of the increase in population in the U.S. occurred in the suburbs.[213] Men and women fled the world of the Cold War into a sort of isolation designed particularly "for the children": security, health, good schools, comfort, "normality." This move presents a picture of intensified privatism, of a deliberate attempt to depend on the family for all satisfactions, indeed, meaning in life. Wider responsibilities, let alone goals of social change, are abandoned for a life defined in terms of what were once considered means to those ends—a reasonable standard of living, education. The house with the most fashionable furnishings and food, the children with the best grades, teeth, and backswings, now exemplify "the good life."

Certainly fleeing the cities meant, for women, fleeing opportunities for full-time careers and political involvement, just as it meant welcoming opportunities for consumerism as a full-time activity.[214] However, perhaps the new numbers of married women who entered the work force during the latter half of the 1940s, the 1950s, and the 1960s (ever larger numbers of them the mothers of young children)[215] were not thinking in terms of full-time careers. Degler concludes that "in spite of the transformation after World War II, women's relations to the family remained as primary as central as it had ever been . . . . The work . . . is clearly subordinated to the needs of the family; in fact, the work is often entered into for the purpose of supporting the family, rather than increasing women's autonomy within the family."[216]

The work of neo-Freudians and sociologists in the 1940s, who have been blamed frequently for their conservative influence on women's image in those years,[217] was indeed used to legitimate the "return home" of the 1950s. This return, and psychological theorizing on it, fostered the hyperindividualism described in the preceding chapter. This was itself a sign of the fragmentation of individualism. It is still easy to view the 1950s drive for security as far less a psychological than a social phenomenon: Whatever the attempt to subordinate the work to the family, to narrow the gaps between the worlds of home, schools, play, friendship, or the generations, it was not successful. The role conflicts experienced by women in the 1950s and increasingly throughout the decades that followed were not fantasy productions; they were historical developments. Nevertheless, in the latter half of the 20th century, as in the 19th century, popular women's fiction has dealt with the problem of integration through images drawn from the inner world of fantasy.

The rise of the "new gothic" parallels the move to suburbia. These books began to be mass produced in paper in the 1950s, and reached the height of their popularity in the 1960s and early 1970s. They have since been equalled in numbers, on the supermarket book racks and in secondhand bookstores, by two other genres of popular women's fiction which resemble them in several ways: the Harlequin Romance, and the "new" historical romance.[218] All three types are formula fiction, unlike many of the books discussed in Chapter Four. In fact, the "new gothic" received this name because it harked back to a plot device of the "old gothic."[219] It begins, typically, with a dramatic and daring journey which lands the heroine ultimately at a large and gloomy house. Otherwise, however, her travelling is of a new sort. Here, as in Chapter Three, the stories follow so regular a pattern that it can be outlined precisely.

Though each heroine is on a specific quest, each of these journeys is an escape into unknown space. These young women cross oceans and continents and class and cultural barriers, in the attempt to uncover a secret of the past, sometimes related to their husbands' families, sometimes to their own. Each heroine places herself constantly in danger; she may be close to death more than once before the dénouement. Thus she exhibits what has been called "justified paranoia";[220] she feels she is watched, but doesn't know by whom, so she (secretly) trusts none of the strangers around her. (As Naida, in *Illusion at*

Haven's Edge, must caution herself: "People who constantly view. . . others with suspicion [are]. . . regarded as having sick minds.")

She exhibits also many characteristics which we have not seen in popular women's fiction since the 19th century. She is typically childish in appearance, and sometimes in behavior, and prone to feelings of unreality. She is often ill, or else recovering from some illness or accident, which may have caused amnesia, either partial or total. Naturally she is orphaned, from early childhood, by the loss of at least one parent, usually her mother. When it is not her mother—and this is a new theme of some interest, as we will see—her mother is presented as selfish or irresponsible, or at least impossibly beautiful.[221] When her father is living, the heroine has been housekeeper or nurse for him, and has idolized him, despite his all-too-obvious impracticality and ineffectuality. Sometimes she is recently bereaved of both her parents, or widowed, divorced, or jilted.

Thrown, then, on her own resources, or early stimulated to develop them, she has invariably aspired to a real, full-time career. This may be in medicine, teaching, archaeology (a favorite), or history. She may write biography, design or model clothes, deal in antiques (another favorite), or catalogue private libraries of rare books. She makes, then, far more determined efforts than previous heroines to develop what the Jungians call her contrasexual self, the traditionally masculine qualities of initiative, courage, objectivity. She wants to develop her interests and skills, but something prevents her: She will leave any job at a moment's notice if any member of her family asks for her help. In *Call in the Night*, *Nun's Castle*, and *Dark Island* the heroines respond to the needs of sisters and a brother, in *Edge of Glass* the heroine is told her estranged grandmother needs her. She promptly walks out on her first big chance to become a film actress to go to her, musing, "If I had to say in words why I had come, I could not have found them."

Therefore it is no great surprise when, at the end of these stories, all but a fraction of these heroines' men demand that they should not work. "I have given up nursing now," comments Diane in *Mansion of Evil*, "because David says he doesn't want his fiancée to work, and besides there is so much to be done before the wedding. And since both Robyn and Martha agree, why what else can I do?" (Robyn is David's child, Martha is Diane's future mother-in-law.)

It is tempting to say, at this point, that we are dealing here with a case of cultural lag: a convention of fictional form, on its last legs, produced and consumed in so perfunctory a fashion that deep unconscious participation is precluded, and superficially adapted to the times—by the themes of exotic travel and the prestigious jobs. But the explanation of this cultural lag is to be found beneath the fictional surface. These fictional young women see strength and know-how as David's, or Roy's, or Gerald's, rather than as possibly their own. Why? We saw in Chapter Four how fathers who are weak and impractical seem to be the rule in 20th century popular women's fiction. A girl's sense of her own competence, as well as her image of herself as sexually attractive, may be aided by the presence of a strong, supportive father. If her father cannot help, she is—in Jungian terms—prone to the form of animus possession which leads to "a strange passivity and paralysis of all feeling, or a deep insecurity that can lead almost to a sense of nullity. . . ."[222] We will soon see several examples of this condition.

Here is the typical father of this group of stories: "A very special man was James Camden. I doubt that one in a hundred could have done what he did. Raise a daughter by himself, with no help whatsoever. True, he had his limitations, his faults. But they were the sort *which only adults notice*; an indifference to the presumed benefits of hard work and a tendency to daydream" [emphases added] (*Secret of the Locket*). Even a father who tries to raise a daughter to be an adult will fail, unless, as I have said, the child's identification with her mother is such as to stimulate such development. And the mothers in these stories, as we will see, are the sort to be rescued from, rather than identified with—though these fathers are even less able than fathers in early 20th century stories to perform the rescue operation.

In *The Daughters of Ardmore Hall* (originally published in 1948 with the title *The Schoolmaster's Daughters*, reprinted in 1967), Truda's father takes his first thoroughly independent action since marriage to the selfish, demanding mother of the story, and dies as a consequence. He does extract a deathbed promise from Truda that she will leave home, mother, and the spoiled, beautiful sister for whom she is in the habit of sacrificing her own needs. But that is as much as she can manage. Anna's father, in *The Secret Woman*, leaves her with her severe and peculiar Aunt Charlotte, while he and Anna's lovely mother go off to India, saying it will be "a worthwhile experience because it [teaches] one to be self-reliant, to face up to life, to stand on one's own feet; he had a stock of clichés to meet occasions like this." His letter to her upon the death, in India, of her mother, is similarly unconsoling, and Anna feels trapped in her aunt's house.

In the absence of both mother and father, these heroines go in search of them. In *Sleeping Tiger*, Selina is told she has developed "an obsession about fathers," and in fact she does escape the house and fly to the other end of Europe, to find the father she believes to be still living. She finds a man resembling her father's picture on a Spanish island; he is the man she eventually marries. It just takes her a little while to teach him not to regard her as a child. One heroine sums up this pattern rather neatly: "Adoring her father as she had, Marcia felt she could hardly have asked for a husband who would better suit her than Jerome" (*The Moonflower*). Jerome does not turn out to be suitable; Marcia must eventually find a *more dependable* man, in order to go living in her childhood fantasy world. Part of the explanation for her inability (and the inability of other heroines) to escape from this fantasy is to be found in their lack of relationship with their mothers. The mothers in these stories are very different from the practical-minded, conventional mothers of Chapter Four.

II. The Comparison of Images

Columbella is very explicit here. "Two months ago Helen Abbott, my mother, had died suddenly and left me alone and free of my bondage," the heroine states. "I had loved her a great deal, and sometimes I had hated her . . . . Often enough my mother had told me that I was born to spinsterhood and the service of others . . . . Men frightened me, she used to say—she who was never afraid of any man! How would I not believe her when I was too young to know any better? But now, though I was no longer a child, and though Helen was gone, I had not yet learned how to still her teasing voice . . . . I could remember envying girls I knew who could use that wonderfully affectionate American word, 'Mommy.' A word that was never permitted to me."

It is sometimes possible for a heroine to escape unaided (except by a man) from this sort of dominance by a mother—or the fantasy image of a mother—who is beautiful, sexual, and only aware of her daughter as a potential rival. The mother of *Secret of the Locket*, whose love story with the heroine's father is "ideal," looks "shallow, even silly" in her girlhood picture. The beautiful mother of *Edge of Glass* is disowned by her family for running away with the heroine's father, and bearing their child out of wedlock. Anna of *The Secret Woman* has another such mother: For her, "everything was dominated by my mother, the most beautiful being in the world." Her mother dies of cholera in India. So involved is Anna with her fantasies that she says she "idealized her beauty. . . when she was alive I could imagine myself growing like her. After she was dead I could not." Yet she achieves for herself by the end of the book, "plain homely Anna" as she still sees herself, just enough self-confidence to respond to a man's love. The mother of Charlotte in *The Sea House* is not only beautiful but unconventional, critical, and unmaternal, and in her presence Charlotte says she does not like herself. However, "she was Tamara. I was Charlotte. We had survived too many turbulences. . . to do more than temporarily strain a bond that would hold us fast as long as either of us lived." Yet Charlotte can, finally, trust herself to love, saying, "I was afraid of myself. . . that you were getting a bad bargain." In *The Turquoise Mask*, the heroine's father finds her looking at a mysterious miniature painting, which she resembles, though she says *she* is "no beauty." Her father tells her "That was a women I once knew. She was worthless—wicked!. . . You're not going to be like her if I can help it. . . ." "I will be like her if I want to!" Amanda responds, and the story is of her determination to prove that her mother was not wicked. She discovers her mother had a child which she gave up before marriage, but she clears her of the other charges of adultery and murder. Then she can love Gavin.

However, in *Columbella* the heroine cannot confront issues so directly, and must work out her attachment to the dominating maternal ideal through another's similar predicament, before she can begin to surmount the "barriers" to love. The girl Lelia, like Jessica's younger self, has to contend against a mother whose sexual attractiveness is competitive. Again there is the comparison of images: Lelia, in the dress Jessica has chosen for her, stares in the mirror and says "I don't know. . . ." Jessica responds, "That's because you're seeing you, instead of Catherine. Your mother couldn't wear this dress." Lelia wears the dress to the ball, where Catherine attempts to humiliate her daughter by dancing with her—"Catherine would know very well how to make her look awkward and foolish"—but Jessica prevents it. "I had been there. I could feel what was happening along my own nerves." In preventing the girl from going to her mother, she acquires some self-confidence of her own, but not yet enough to live on. After the party we find her staring at herself in a mirror, at an "unfamiliar" face, and when she speaks aloud to herself, the voice is "critical" and tells her that her love must be unrequited. Lelia must be completely rescued, by her mother's death, before love can be trusted. The confusion of self-image with mother-image is illustrated also in the opening pages of *The Stranger in the Mirror*, where another Jessica confronts herself in the mirror, "this Jessica who'd *really done something awful this time* [italics mine] . . . . The face in the mirror belonged to a woman at least forty years old . . . . She ran screaming into the empty hall."

The confrontation with one's resemblance to mother does not always produce so violent a reaction. But it is never a pleasant discovery, as it was, for example, for the heroines of domestic fiction. These incessant comparisons, in which the daughter always comes out as *less desirable than mother*, appear to symbolize an entirely different phenomenon than those earlier assertions of exact similarity, or even than the self-defeating "mirror stares" of early 20th century women's fiction. It is tempting to suggest that we have here (since sexual desirability and maturity are clearly at issue) a symbol of the oedipal confrontation, with daughter always losing to mother, and arrested permanently at that stage of her development. However, I think we have to go even farther back than this to explain the persistent low estimation of themselves these heroines maintain.

III. Images of the Body

For women trying to grow up after World War II, experience of the physical self is more complicated (if possibly also more enjoyable) in its expression than it was for earlier generations. In Chapter Four we saw heroines more or less fixated on the question of their physical attractiveness to men. Very little exploration of their sexual responsiveness was yet admitted to their writing, for all their use of the term "passion." Kinsey, and the "sexual revolution" of the 1960s, have made the question of female sexuality impossible to ignore for writers of romantic suspense fiction.

According to Freudian theory (and clinical experience), girl children can worry about whether or not their bodies are whole. As Greenacre puts it, "The body areas which are . . . most significant in comparing and contrasting the establishing individual recognition of the body self . . . are the face and the genitals."[223] We will see how obsessively the young women in these stories compare and contrast their faces to Mother's face. This is fairly easy to write openly about. The other obsession, a fear that Mother has not provided them with quite "everything," or the resentment caused by such a fear, must be translated into classic "gothic" imagery in these stories, where young women cannot escape but must search old houses for a secret treasure.

In *Nun's Castle*, the missing sister's box of doll furniture is discovered with "every tiny piece . . . broken . . . each piece of fragile elegance deliberately broken in two." We later find the culprit was the nurse, the "deadly, deadly Nesta, destroying all she touched." In *Hunter's Green*, the act that finished the chance for love between child-heroine and stepmother was the latter's disposal of a favorite teddy bear. "I flew at Janet like a demon child . . . In my bedroom I laid about me with a will for a few minutes, breaking what came to hand, and kicking things in damaged confusion." Before the stepmother can do more harm, the child will do it to herself! (This pattern recurs in the later life of these heroines.) Similarly, in *Mansion in Miniature*, Crystal's roomful of miniatures is "smashed," "an act of violent obscenity"—and though Karen's first thought is that "a man was responsible for this," in fact "it was Mother who broke them . . . she went on a rampage. She would have destroyed the dollhouse if there'd been time." As one writer on the subject suggests, "the 'silent' organ of the girl is symbolized in the accounts of dolls who are alive only when no one looks,"[224] and troublesome sexual feelings in girls are often displaced onto care for favorite dolls. (Of course, girls' organs would be neither "silent" nor so troublesome if mothers did not make a secret of them.)[225]

For the heroine in *The Moonflower*, whose daughter, like herself, believes in a "wickedness inside," freedom and self-acceptance cannot come through self-knowledge. It is too late for that: Instead the plot must proceed through the almost ritualistic mutilation and death of another woman. The scapegoat

Hiroshima maiden in that story hangs herself; when the heroine of *The Golden Unicorn* discovers the shadow figure Stacia dead, nearby is "the carton of doll's heads . . . with only a few of the heads left in it." These are left over from Stacia's childhood habit of breaking up her dolls. Stacia's mother rejected her from the beginning, in order to paint. "I took to breaking up my dolls," says Stacia to her, "Maybe because I couldn't get through to you." The heroine of this story, Courtney, listens to this and comments mildly to the mother, Judith (whom Courtney fears at one point is *her* real mother), "At least you've put those broken dolls to good use . . . . They seem to have become a sort of signature for your paintings . . . and they lend a haunting quality." (Earlier Courtney has spoken of the "unsettling air of fantasy imposed on reality" in these paintings.) Later when Judith is painting a "Stacia-doll" she tells Courtney "Stacia poisons everything she touches. She destroys." It is the mother who is destructive, but Stacia has obviously accepted this projection of her mother's image onto herself. (As Riviere describes this mechanism, the daughter, fearing her own womanhood as destructive, turns "in dread from that side of life and develops a masculine role.")[226] Her Uncle John teaches her boys' games and, as she puts it, rescues her "from all that feminine nonsense girls are doomed to." The daughter in *The Moonflower* also smashed dolls.

At this story's end, Courtney, purged of the poison of womanhood by Stacia's death, finds her own mother, and says she has come to the end of her search. However, we have two pages to go, and Courtney does not say "I had come home indeed" until her lover Evan's arms are around her. The successful search for the mother is a rare plot element in the story of romantic suspense, and when it does occur, it invariably ends with this double dénouement. The discovery of a gratifying mother, rather than a hostile, devouring one, is not enough to still these heroines' doubts about themselves. They need more than that. But what?

IV. The Perilous Journey

Almost no story in the genre fails to open with the prospect or fact of a considerable journey. Each heroine attempts the escape into space, travelling far on her ambiguous errand. In the sample I am using in this chapter, the heroines travel to New York and California (from Chicago), Ireland and Scotland (from London), and to England (three of them), Spain (two of them), Hong Kong, Majorca, Italy (again, two), Paris, the Midi (two), Haiti, and all over the New England states—from various points west. Rare indeed is the heroine who can find what she needs by staying in one place[227]; the flight from the emptiness or unreality of their lives toward something to fill it or make it real is irresistible, although they are remarkably unsuccessful, at first, in their search. In *A Visit After Dark*, the heroine returns from a stay in a mental hospital to the town in Texas to which her marriage had taken her, only to find her physical double living with her husband, in her place. Naida, in *Illusion at Haven's Edge*, comes "home" still without the memory of the crucial hours in which she is suspected by everyone but her father to have committed a double murder. And, so on. Like heroines in popular women's fiction from its beginnings, they have trouble distinguishing self from other, but these young women keep moving, imagining a hope; around the corner of the next dark corridor, recognition and the fulfilling miracle will take place.[228] Courtney, who in *The Golden Unicorn* goes in quest of her real parents, has long had an "amazing success" as a freelance writer, but has turned from this public role in despair. She watches a TV interview of herself, and thinks "it had lost all reality for me. Indeed, I sometimes wondered what reality there had ever been for me in my whole life." Virginia, in *Cry Witch*, says "What I need is to feel that my mother really loved me, in spite of the fact that she chose to leave me," and sets out to prove that her mother's supposed suicide was, in fact, a murder. The heroine in *Edge of Glass* is not only responding to her family's "need," she is also in search of her (recently deceased) mother's precious crystal goblet, "the Culloden Cup"—a grail quest into the maternal mystery indeed.

I have called the quests on which these fictional young women embark "ambiguous." The appropriate psychological terms for their state of mind is ambivalence, for they are involved in flight *from and toward* the regressive pull of the primal maternal image.[229] For all their defensive strivings and successes, they want back the bliss of babyhood, the oneness with the maternal flesh of which they never had enough. They are drawn back to this dangerous mystery, in a mixture of fascination and repulsion, under a number of guises. The "Culloden Cup" is one example, the dark and gloomy house itself another. A character in one novel would be "destroyed" if she had to leave her house (*The Golden Unicorn*). In other cases, the house is an image of a terrified, defensive sterility. In *Nun's Castle*, the heroine is called "the Snow Queen in [her] maiden's castle . . . ." One young woman dreams of her home as deserted, overgrown with weeds, harboring "no living creature but me" (*Quin's Hide*).

In *Across the Common*, Louise does not know "where home is." Her husband remarks, "You haven't transferred your home yet . . . and they [her family of women] make you ill." It takes her most of the book to discover her childhood home is "just a house," and still, at the story's end, she is struck with "a terrible pain" when her aunt packs her bags and strips her bed and leaves on it "the zipped-up poodle . . . flat as a woman after childbirth." Louise has managed to leave Mother, but not easily.

In a thriller called *The Cottage*, a woman harbors her lover in a replica in miniature of the big house in which she lives. The young man finds "something repellant here." The woman's botched affair with him is what might be expected of a woman who has not developed a differentiated self-image but regards herself as an inferior simulation of a mother she dare not compete with sexually. Like Charlotte in *The Sea House*, she is "caught and trapped" in Mother's house; like Selina in *Nun's Castle* she dreams of "locks and bolts and deep dark dungeons."

The attempt to escape these houses, and the other dangerous houses that these young women cannot resist entering and re-entering, is doomed to fail for two reasons. The most obvious, of course, is their very childishness. For example, Virginia, in *Cry Witch*, looks "closer to her fourteenth birthday than to the twenty-fourth she could celebrate in June," in *A Visit After Dark* Mary is "slight as a child," and in *Sleeping Tiger*, Selina is described as "too young even to be pretty." One heroine, Karen, in *Mansion in Miniature*, is, by profession, a successful dollhouse and miniature dealer. The significance of this is easily summed up in quotation: "I wanted more than ever I'd wanted anything to become small enough to enter the dreaming loveliness of the dollhouse . . . an uncontrollable urge, an unquenchable need . . . a child's wish." Karen's beautiful sister, Crystal, "had escaped into miniatures because childhood was the only escape she had," because, as another character remarks to Karen, "no use trying to fight Mother . . . ."

Yet the regressive pull toward childhood is as terrifying as it is seductive. It is in the very kitchen, "the safest room in the house," that one heroine has her "private hell of blackness and fear of death"—the asthma attack, which is, in analytic interpretation, a stifled cry for the rejecting Mother who does not answer.[230] Suffocation, replicating that earliest emergency of the hungrily crying infant, threatens nearly every heroine in these books. She may be asthmatic or prone to obsessive screaming attacks. In *Visit After Dark*, Mary "had a momentary vision of snow falling, drowning her, suffocating her . . . . Her screams faded and grew again. She was lost in it, lost in it, lost . . . ." "She must be insane to stand screaming at nothing in an empty room," another character comments. She may be claustrophobic, as in *The Sea House*: "I can't breathe. I'm choking . . . . This hole in the earth . . . set loose in me a frantic, animal fear." The heroine's brother is asthmatic in this novel and so is the bad first wife in *The Secret Woman*. Someone may try to hang her (*Illusion at Haven's Edge*), strangle her (*Call in the Night* and *Dark Island*), drown her (*Golden Unicorn, Mansion of Evil*, and *Nun's Castle*), smother her (*Mansion in Miniature* and *Mansion of Evil*), bury her alive (*Shadows Waiting, The Severing Line* and *Lament for Four Brides*), or she may dream someone has buried her alive (*Cry Witch*). In *The Daughters of Ardmore Hall*, the mother actually strangles and then drowns one of the daughters. This is rare. But equally rare is a heroine who does not make much of her primitive physical terror of the older women who threaten her. The heroine of *Quin's Hide* is uniquely heroic in this respect; she quells the "bone-deep throb of fear" her stepmother, whom she calls Mother, inspires. "My breath came easier. Why had I imagined I was afraid of her!" The answer, by the way, is given some pages earlier: "I was afraid of the impossible paragon of womanhood she presented to me," and later, by "Mother" herself, "I never loved you! Whatever gave you that idea!"

Another significant set of images here are those concerning households of women, without any men to assist in rescuing the heroines. In *Sleeping Tiger*, "a man . . . had scarcely ever entered the house." Selina has "no father, no grandfather, no uncle, no brother. Nobody." In the house of her three aunts, Louise "can meet them as a child, but not as a woman." Here, in "mama's" house, they have "disposed of their men," so that a real man is an extraordinary appearance. At one point, Aunt Rose is compared to the Aztec Goddess, Eater of Filth—for she keeps the shameful family secret of grandfather's sex crime. It is not at all fear of men that we see here, however, but rather of Mother as the devourer and mutilator—and no Father anywhere, to save the daughter from her.

These heroines, then, present a picture of something more complex than role-conflict. Their sense of self appears damaged, as is shown by an intense body-consciousness that is painful in several ways. First, these heroines find themselves both sexually and generally inadequate. They are not as attractive as their mothers, or as the shadow figures in these fictions, who are sexier, and openly so. The heroines are also not as independent nor as competent in their careers or tasks as they need to be. They always need help. Both these lacks can be related to their fathers' inability to help them grow up, much in the same way I described that situation in Chapter Four. Secondly, these heroines feel that their bodies are like their mothers': mysterious, dangerous, and seductive bodies. This feeling *cannot be yielded to*, for it is deeply confused with the desire to be an infant again, and this threatens the fragile ego boundaries of these heroines. All of this imagery seems to reflect a narcissistic self-absorption even greater than that reflected in fiction of the earlier half of the century, and also a trait of the infantile personality type which was not evident in the earlier 20th century stories (but which we did see in domestic fiction; in mothers, not daughters).

Nevertheless, these heroines have their way of dealing with their conflicts, and it is not the denial nor the busy displacement we saw in Chapter Four; no, they always try to find the secret hidden in the maternal mystery. The chief obstacle in the way of each heroine is herself.

V. The Image of the Other Self

The heroine of a story of romantic suspense has, as I have already suggested, very bad luck. I have mentioned some of the variety of forms it takes: accident, illness, sensational errors in judgment of other people. She is also unable to say no when asked to perform a different or confusing task. She gets herself into dreadful messes, in fact. Yet all of this makes psychological sense when we observe that the precipitating misfortune of all others is the loss of an important "love object" and an uncompleted work of mourning. Given this, we can understand these young women as suffering from a residue of conscious and unconscious guilt. We can also begin to understand why they flee from unfulfilled lives, if the "image of death is a feeling of emptiness or absence."[231] This pattern of a flight which is not a flight is repeated again and again in these stories, preventing individual accomplishment, of course, but also causing clear and present trouble.

For example, in a story called *The Water Horse*, Charlotte takes a holiday trip with her beloved father (her mother died when Charlotte was six months old) in which she senses "a strange urgency in their progress. For it was too concentrated, too much of a good thing. She would not admit it, but it was with an odd sensation of release that she returned to work." Sure enough, it is the last time she sees him alive, and a mysterious letter he leaves behind hints at murder. Charlotte falls ill, acquiring a "wasted face and haunted eyes," and we discover her some months later, incognito on a park bench, "morose, totally self-absorbed . . . blank eyes not seeming to absorb any light." Her animus-possessed quest for the murderer is interrupted by episodes of weakness, lethargy, and plain witlessness, not to speak of fainting spells. After one of these she speaks of being able to hear the Furies, and it is only the kiss of her true-love that can transform her completely, at novel's end, from the "blank-eyed zombie of an hour ago."

Another young woman becomes a "zombie" midway through her search into her family's criminal secrets, at the mere suggestion that her husband (whom she has left) could leave *her*: "never, even in a dream, or during an [asthmatic] attack had I felt such cold terror. To be alone, and alone because of someone else's action . . . the safe world around me dissolved and shifted . . . words like *death, loss, love* rang . . . with the exact melancholy of bells tolling under deep water" (*Across the Common*). Repressed fantasies of guilt have another even more inconvenient effect on these heroines. In *Stranger in the Mirror*, Tracy is totally amnesiac; in *Illusion at Haven's Edge*, Naida is amnesiac for the period during which she is supposed to have committed a double murder of parental figures; in *Cry Witch*, Gigi can't remember the childhood trauma that makes her unable to love; in *Nun's Castle*, Selina can't even remember whether she's been married or not: "I knew I had puzzled the doctors," she comments. "It was as if [my sickness] had created a second me, a sick twin, who went around living a life on her own . . . . I felt as if I were bleeding somewhere."

The unconscious operations of guilt and self-punishment become even more complicated where the death is that of neither parent, but of the shadow self *as double*, which Selina's fantasy illustrates. Fantasies of a double are persistent in the narcissistic personality.[232] This way of imagining inadmissible parts of the self is a new convention. First, a double may appear as a sibling. In *Mansion in Miniature* it is a younger and more beautiful sister. "You can't escape me, Karen, we are twins of the psyche, united in our souls," Crystal says. That night "she . . . killed herself, and it was all my [Karen's] fault. My parents no longer stared at me from behind a cloud. They confronted me openly . . . . The wrath of Moses was on their faces . . . . I would never forgive myself . . . . I'd punish myself . . . ." And so on; the heroine, again, cannot accept love because of her guilt. "Whenever I saw Hugo, I'd feel the need to atone," she says. The story ends with her plans to build "a monument" to her sister. Similarly, in *The Severing Line*, the heroine rejects "happiness," saying "guilt, more guilt. It seemed to me the only bond that held Jud and me together as we viewed the total wreck of Claire's life."

Another Claire, in *Call in the Night*, abandons her career and flies to London and Paris to help her irresponsible younger sister. Lucy, of *Quin's Hide*, tries to rescue her half-brother Robin from criminal involvements. Janet, in *Dark Island*, travels illegally to Haiti in search of her younger brother Peter, made a zombie by voodoo or perhaps "a mind-slowing drug." The search is "all I have to live for," she claims. Peter's death, and her subsequent desire for revenge, are described in detail. "I glanced in the mirror and was shocked at the expression on my face. It was evil . . . I wanted [his murderess] to face a hypnotized goat and watch her be told her soul was being transferred into the goat . . . . I wanted all the evil things I could think of . . . ." As is usual in such cases, only Janet's true-love can cajole her out of bitter self-reproach and self-destructive action. When there is no lover's voice to be heard, the heroine cannot possibly sort out her emotions. "I lived in a bemused state for weeks afterward," reports the heroine of *The Secret Woman*, after the title character's death. "I kept going over parts of my life with Chantel . . . to me she had been the sister I had always wanted . . . . The murderess was the secret woman in her, the woman I should never have believed existed if she herself had not shown her to me . . . . My life seemed empty without her." The daughter of the villainess in *Columbella* includes herself and the heroine in guilt for her mother's death: "It's my fault! . . . I should have known you'd do nothing to help her."

In *The Sea House*, yet another Charlotte has secretly refused to accept the fact of her long-lost twin brother's death: "Loneliness was no new enemy to me; I had been acquainted with it all my life . . . . But now . . . my enemy had caught me off guard . . . I had floundered in a sea of desolation as enveloping as that which must attack a forsaken child." When her brother Esmond, who was not dead, does die (in her arms) she feels that "the misjudgments, the prejudices, the blindness was mine!" and that "out of disaster, violence and death, love could not flower. I was possessed by a dark, sticky, down-dragging guilt that if I'd never come to Glissing, Esmond would still be alive . . . . Against reason and logic I felt it was I and I alone who was responsible for his death." For three days, she fights her way out of "the guilt and shock in which [she'd] come near drowning," before she can bring herself to send for her lover after all. Similarly, Lucy in *Quin's Hide* feels "one pain that transcended all other, irrational, maybe immoral, a great yawning of compulsive pity" for Robin, and she so automatically assumes that his murder of her lover's mother has spoiled her life that she cannot recognize a proposal when she hears one. These young women cannot save, can only continue to mourn, these shadows of their own unrealized beauty, selfishness, adventurousness, even violence.

Though the bad part-self is eliminated, the bad mother image remains, imposing its burden. In fact, if these young women are not disposed to blame themselves for the deaths in their families, others will do it for them: Lucy's stepmother and sister blame her for Robin's death; Truda is suspected of having murdered her sister Charlotte; Naida, having been framed for two murders, is held guilty by *her* stepmother and sister for those, and for her father's subsequent heart failure. And so on. It is significant that it is images of the bad mother who do the blaming. The self-punishing parodies of mourning which these young women act out can be interpreted in two possible ways, the second underlying the first. A daughter has to be punished for growing up; also, the poison-mother image, incorporated in early infancy, cannot be easily repressed by a daughter, so that young women (however unconsciously) regard themselves as similarly dangerous. As we have seen, the danger is very great, for the "infantile or 'mother' superego is of the utmost harshness and cruelty."[233]

This fantasy of the cruel part-self is fended off in these stories by yet another narcissistic image of the double. Many of these heroines try to rescue younger siblings who are what they themselves do not dare to be; many more rescue desperately damaged and endangered children, who know a secret.

Although even in the costume fictions of this period no heroine takes work as a governess out of economic necessity, but only in answer to some personal appeal, she very often agrees to take charge of someone else's child. The child is invariably physically ill, mentally disturbed, or both, and the heroine is able to heal both disorders and sometimes rescue the girl or boy from attempted murder as well. For example, in *Night of the Bonfire*, Kay, fleeing from a lover who has killed her love "in the wasteland of his possessiveness," says she takes a new job "for [his] mental stability as much as for her own peace of mind," 300 miles away. There, she is to catalogue a library, but quickly discovers that the small girl in the family is afflicted with a violently selfish and jealous mother, and that the father is "afraid for . . . [his] only child." When the mother is murdered, it is the child who first discovers the body, and it falls to Kay to deal with the situation. "A wrong word, a false move, and Ginny would run from her. Worse, she could escape from reality in the withdrawal of autistic despair."

Other women have even more awkward tasks. In *The Master of Penrose* and *Mansion of Evil*, the children have already witnessed scenes of horror before the story opens. Sarah, in the former story, discovered her mother with her lover, and was then shut up in the dark for hours; Sarah does not speak until nearly the end of the book. Robyn, in the latter story, found her drowned mother's body. In *Castle Barebane*, Val takes over the care of both of her psychotic brother's children (their mother is dead); the semi-autistic girl is drowned, though the boy is saved. In the *Voice of the Dolls*, the child Jennie has heard all the ugly secrets of her family, and dramatizes them with her set of puppet-dolls. The heroine, Sarah, after overhearing this from the next garden, signs on as her governess. In *Illusion at Haven's Edge*, Charles has witnessed the murder of his mother by his father, and Naida, despite her own considerable problems, must cope with this.

Regularly, the heroines who save these children with their terrible secret knowledge are rewarded with marriage to the child's father or uncle, replacing the bad mother of each story—this pattern occurs also in *The Silence of Herondale*, *Night of the Bonfire*, and *The Stranger in the Mirror*. This formula of escape through the destruction of evil-self-as-mother image, and the reconstruction of a new all-good family for the child, is also a way for these young women to escape the danger of their own bodies. In those cases where the heroine acquires a child by proxy, she is magically enabled to become the woman she does not dare to become, in any real way. Making an "instant family" in this fashion does not, it is hardly necessary to say, symbolize growing up. It is, rather, an image of motherhood as an act of acquisition, far more like the Whole New Wardrobe convention of Chapter Four than any confrontation with the terrifying potentials of the self. This theme of the "legitimation" of the frightening female body (with its invisibilities, its dangerous global sensations, the unsconscious fears of injury or even of already being wounded which it arouses—not to speak of the fear that the inside is full of badness)[234] is still present in stories where the rescued child is the woman's own.

In *One Way to Venice*, the child has been released for adoption at birth. His mother not only finds him but becomes reconciled with his father; together, the three of them escape a mass-murder plot, escaping a trap in a cave which was an ammunition dump! "Dear God, what a fool I've been," Julia is still saying at the end of the novel. In *The Moonflower* the father, Jerome, attempts to take his child away from the mother (who has followed him to Tokoyo) by teaching the little girl of the "wicked things human beings [do] to each other," and that she "must never trust anyone." Mother and daughter are symbolically freed to go home with a new husband and father by the suicide of a horribly disfigured Japanese woman. Resolution, then, is achieved in these books in the same way that it is achieved in earlier 20th century popular fiction. For the bad part of the split self, there is a death so that the good part can live happily ever after, obeying a good husband, and the promptings of the "mother" superego, which are never entirely exorcised.

Finding a good husband becomes as difficult as it was in 19th century fiction: These heroines, like the earlier ones, can neither identify the bad in men nor trust their feelings for the good in them. (The heroine of *One Way to Venice* trusts her man, finally, only because she "must.") In case a heroine does have some self-confidence in these matters, the very strength of her defenses against dependency blocks her vision: To a proposal of marriage, for example, Lucy of *Quin's Hide* replies briskly, "It's reaction. Tomorrow you'll regret your noble offer. Not to worry. I won't hold you to ransom." Sarah, in *The Voice of the Dolls*, comments "Rachel said I was in love with you. What nonsense!" Andrea, in *The Severing Line*, says of the man she loves: "Well, worst had not yet come to worst. I found my way without Judson Cole's help." Kate, in *The Master of Penrose*, responds to the passion of her beloved with the comment, "You're either mad or drunk... or both. But there's no time for it."

VI. Images of Men

On the other hand, when these women do give in, they are like earlier 20th century heroines in that they abandon their defenses completely and indiscriminately. In Jungian terms, they fall victim to a projection of the unintegrated animus, in the image of demon lover, an intensely strong and sexually dominating character type. Suddenly, after a lapse of a century, women's fiction includes a male lover or husband whose silences and secrets make him mysterious[235] but whose dominance, once accepted, may yield an exclusive marvel of tenderness. This fictional type sketches a redemption motif: Men may *seem* to be brutes, bullies, thieves, and murderers—but *get them in private*, and they are really perfectly sweet. That this formula neatly supports the suburban collective dream (if hardly its reality) is not surprising. That it remains formulaic in ever more wildly dramatized form in the historical romances of the late 1970s is rather more disconcerting. A particularly gruesome example may perhaps suffice: In Marilyn Harris's *This Other Eden* (New York: Avon, 1978), our hero has our (stubbornly virginal) heroine stripped and flogged, bound to a great black oaken stake in his courtyard, while he hides upstairs in his bedroom. Of course these two subsequently found a dynasty together (permitting a dynasty of "Eden" novels). Though the heroines of novels of romantic suspense choose the same sort of men to love, they do not make a style of resistance. The heroine of a historical romance obdurately refuses to let her *spirit* be broken by her beloved's treatment of her, even after she has yielded to him sexually. Yet unfailingly she too chooses a beloved who tries to dominate her utterly, and who finally does so.

I have been arguing that American women, socialized from birth to life-long guilt-ridden dependency, transfer their dependencies from their mothers to the men they marry. Even a sporadic recognition that men are childish, too, has not seemed to alter that dependence. The passionate affirmation of male power imaged in the heroes [236] of popular women's fiction since 1950 suggests no significant change in the pattern. [237]

The murderous anger of the heroine is of course contained as well as punished in advance, in fantasies of the indifferent, strong, dangerous, driven hero. The terror which is the complement of that anger is alleviated by the ultimate "reward" of a private moment's tenderness. "Mommy's sorry; Mommy didn't really mean it." If most of those who explain such rage and such terror psychologically are correct, it can result from the confusion and timidity of America's child-rearing practices since World War II, that have failed to provide the ego strength necessary for competitive effort. A non-competitive personality is one defeated by persistent infantile fantasies of reprisal. [238]

Positive identification cannot take place even where a suitable role model is available. The dreadfulness of the maternal image in these stories is, we have seen, a primitive, infantile fantasy, gaining additional power from the sexual competitiveness between women that has been another social feature of the years in question. (Perhaps it has been, as well, the main sort of role-modeling mothers have been doing.) The fear of such competition— indeed of any competition—must be contained or alleviated, for it is intoler-able. In the fiction, a perfect device for containing both is the strong husband. Of course, these heroines usually pick the wrong man first. For example, in *Mansion in Miniature*: "Paul said 'You will marry me soon,' and said it so positively I agreed." That's page 141, where he appears to her "a rock to protect me." On page 178, her *true* love, Hugo, beats Paul up. "If an outside observer had suddenly materialized in the room he would have thought that the villain, not the hero of the piece, had triumphed . . . . Since Paul had been reduced to something for the dump heap, Hugo left him and came to me . . . what I'd always [sic] dreamed of was coming true." Or, in *Night of the Scorpion*, as Josefa responds to Rob: "Her heart was warm, hot, racing. She remembered their kisses . . . she was half in love and knew it." Less than a hundred pages later, she is kissing the good guy, and thinks "For all she knew, she was kissing death . . . . She remembered that she responded to Rob's kiss, too. And still didn't know who was telling the truth."

When Rob turns up, he looks at Josefa "with such hatred as she would never have believed were she not seeing it," and so, "like a miracle" she loves the other man, and in a fight with him Rob topples off a sea cliff. "Follow me now," says her true-love, and "She did exactly what he said." In the *Daughters of Ardmore Hall*, when the good man asks Truda if she is still in love with her husband (who has run off with her shadow figure sister), "She could scarcely speak for anger." "No one ought to trust you," she tells him, later, and even when she admits to herself that she is in love with him, and that "she had distrusted love," she goes right on distrusting it. Of her love for her husband: "It was terrible.... Would her love for Luke be the same— rapturous and brief? She hated herself." In *Call in the Night*, Claire has an even worse difficulty: "I tried to accept the fact that Garth was a murderer but my mind balked at such an idea.... I had already persuaded myself against all the evidence that Garth was innocent." When she goes to talk to him, he lies (to protect her, naturally). "I ran from him, stumbling down the path to the road, and although I would have turned back in a flash if he had called my name he said nothing and I knew then that he was relieved to see me go." A few minutes later, she allows herself to be picked up and driven off by the real killer, because she feels she can't face Garth. This sort of self-evaluation, and this sort of self-destructive behavior, is the norm for these heroines.

The relationship which sums up the theme of all these secondary plots occurs in *Illusions at Haven's Edge*, in which the doctor who has the heroine committed (to save her from prison, we eventually discover) is the man she "must" come to love. At first, "anger...flamed within me whenever I thought of Dr. Roy Duncan, who'd had me committed, though I was cautious not to give evidence of my ire... anger which might be construed as a mental disorder of sorts." But at story's end she is coauthor of a book: "I blush with pleasure when my beloved speaks of his pride in my modest accomplishment. Even now, he is urging me to begin one of my own. I'm sorely tempted." Given a man's quasiparental permission and approval, she can even con- template seeking the world's recognition for her "modest" level of accom- plishment. On the other hand, in *Edge of Glass*, the heroine gives up her ambitions to act, and learns to type and do bookkeeping for her husband; she *does* continue modeling, but for "cake mixes and Marsha's chocolates.... It is gentler work, almost dull, and it does not clutch at me and make me sharp and bad tempered and exhausted, as the other used to.... I am anxious to get home again. Letting go can be a sweet relief." Yet perhaps such conclu- sions compare favorably with those where the future husband commends the heroine for her porridge, as at the end of *The Silence of Herondale*, or her boiled eggs, at the end of *Call in the Night*: The emphasis placed on the specifically nurturant role has its unattractive implications, as we shall see.

Before we come to that topic, we should note one significant variant of the parental role in these stories. In a sizable number of these novels, the plausible and charming deceiver is a very much older man: the heroine's boss in *One Way to Venice*, *The Voice of the Dolls*, *Shadows Waiting*, and *Lament for*

Four Brides. In other stories, (*The Golden Unicorn, Cry Witch*) he is a relative or enjoys a privileged relationship with a relative, though he is a villain. Here, there is no question of mistake in love, though the heroines who succumb to the persuasive personalities of these men would not be doing so, if they could admit their love for the good man. Also, they would be spared some danger: The older man is extremely powerful and manipulative. In *One Way to Venice*, the villain has virtually created the heroine, for example "at the extraordinary finishing school to which he had sent her. At the same time she had learned so many other things. How to speak, how to dress, how to eat; almost, it seemed, how to live." In other cases the plot to kill which these demanding employers invent and put into practice is more prominent in the story, but there is always an initial stage in which the heroine is trying to win his approval. It does not take much imagination to see here a displacement of the fear of an overwhelmingly intrusive mother onto the man, right through the plot devices of months of imprisonment, drugging, murder, and the kidnapping of girl children for which these older men are responsible and (of course) eventually punished, usually by death.

Here, a primitive incomplete bad object is disposed of, so that the heroine is left with the partial object who spoils her. Unable to integrate her images of self, and lose her "good" self-image of passivity and compliance, she merely represses her own aggression and greed, when the villains in the case are killed off. Let us examine this process.

VII. Images of Repressed Greed and Anger

We have already, in earlier chapters, questioned the premise that sexual repression is the most disturbing, or even a very seriously disturbing, element in the psychic life of the writers and readers of popular women's fiction. Object–relations theory has taken us back to a stage beyond the oedipal triangle, and even in this contemporary body of fiction, where various relationships with father figures play a relatively large role, the early relationship with the mother has been much more thematically and imagically prominent. Klein speculates that the girl's urge to fill her inner world with good objects "contributes to the intensity of her introjective processes, which are also reinforced by the receptive nature of her genital."[239] If we are willing to accept that the early psychic experience of girl babies may involve them in a unique experience of the inner self, we can make a connection between the passionate concern of babies with food (and their own greed, and consequent aggression, and consequent guilt) and the concern of young women with their later experiences of passion. What are we to make of the fact that these heroines of popular fiction, anorexic and/or wasted as many of them are, nevertheless describe themselves as greedy—"greedy for love," as one mother figure is called, "*starved for love*," as one heroine claims to be?

Klein says that, before the development of the oedipal stage, the internalized persecuting mother *and* the pressures from body drives can all but squeeze out the ego. She speaks of an "uncontrollably greedy and destructive infant" who "could not develop an individuality of her own" let alone be stimulated by the world of outer reality to substantial intellectual achievement.[240]

This explanation of intellectual inhibition is a fair enough description of the young women we have been reading about. Between their unconscious preoccupation with their bodies' unsolved "mysteries" and their guiltiness, they forget to behave with average common sense, let alone intellectual mastery. As for uncontrollable greed, in at least three of the stories in this group, we have truly startling examples. The disturbed little girl (who dies) in *Castle Barebane*, "wary and timid" with people, "tastes *everything*—if you let her—bark, raw potatoes, ivy leaves, pebbles on the beach . . . onions with marmalade, porridge and pine needles, milk and grass." In *The Voice of the Dolls*, old Mrs. Foster appears with "a wheezing sound like that of an obese spaniel . . . an elderly lady of very great bulk . . . her nose and mouth and small sharp bright eyes, no doubt of normal size in a normally sized face . . . so diminished by the breadth of her cheeks that her face had an odd look of distortion." Later we see her having second helpings of Victorian meals, "her cheeks bulging" with buns bought in the park, complaining that she couldn't do justice to her dinner because her dress was too tight, and also, throwing a tantrum when she is beaten at a game: "With a movement like a spoilt child she tilted the board and spilled the men to the floor."

The "uncontrollably greedy" character in *Night of the Scorpion* is even more frightening. The heroine, Josepha, has been mysteriously summoned to the side of her aging aunt and uncle on their California horse ranch. (Since the age of 12 she has spent summers there; her parents are now both dead. This leaves the aunt as the mother figure.) When Josepha arrives, her uncle explains to her that Aunt Luz's "heart has been giving trouble, and when she . . . overeats . . . well, that retching and straining . . . that brings on the heart. . . . Also, carrying so much weight is a burden on the heart." While this conversation is going on, Aunt Luz is happily helping herself to another "huge slab" of the chocolate cake which Josepha has eaten some of, to be polite. Josepha, who is in medical school, devotes much time and energy in the pages that follow into putting her aunt on a diet; in fact, she freezes all the food, although Joey too is capable of eating "hungrily," unlike most of these romantic heroines. However, the old lady sneaks an entire pizza in the middle of the night, and her heart gives out in the ensuing upset. Yet Joey suspects that someone has poisoned the salad she made, and sets out to prove it. At this point, Joey loses her appetite and trusts no one. Her inheritance of Luz's ranch crushes her with guilt. Of course, the demon lover, Rob, is the poisoner. He killed Luz for the ranch, and drugged all the horses with LSD, in an attempt to kill Joey and her true-love, E. J.[241]

As I have already mentioned, E. J. disposes of this image of a bad object. Now, in theory, the ego—the self that masters reality, and is not trapped in infantile fantasy—grows, when bad objects are expelled.[242] In the fantasy world of these stories, no such thing can happen. Aunt Luz's vomiting from the effects of the poison is what really causes her death. When Joey's imaged bad object, the poisoner and manipulator, is expelled from her world, she immediately loses what appearance of an adult ego she had, and reverts to her childhood love for E. J. "You deserve something more than Mrs. E. J. Barr," he comments, but her response is, "I'd never ask for more." He permits her to continue her medical training however, so they can open a clinic together—he is a veterinarian.

In the popular women's fiction of the 19th century a woman is not marriageable unless she can bring either fortune or wifely capability, or both, to the marriage. This latter qualification, particularly in its aspect of submissiveness (made all the more valuable by the vaunted previous intelligence and independence of the heroine), is what allows these young women of the second half of the 20th century to marry. As one writer on the genre comments, "the only body a woman can inhabit with relative ease is a wife's body, the only 'house' she can finally live in is the 'home' she makes and her husband owns."[243] "Owns" is the operative word here, for her inheritance must be given over to her husband, just as inheritances were transferred in the first collection of novels we looked at. While the shadow selves and bad guys are usually mad with greed, be they first wives, rivals, brothers, mother, or child–self images, the heroine is never greedy—she is all selflessness. She gives the self away.

These young women claim that they have stumbled onto the knowledge of how they have been persecuted, robbed, or cheated, with no real personal interest in the matter at all, and nobly disclaim their rights in anything but a minor share in their husband's lives. They insist that their curiosity was either purely intellectual, or on someone else's behalf (as in *Lament for Four Brides*, where the treasure hunt is for money for an operation for the heroine's paralytic husband), or a matter of loyalty, however mistaken, to someone else—the murdered parent, the disappearing sibling, the traumatized child. They *do not want to own anything*. For example, Charlotte in *The Sea House* absolutely refuses to show her grandmother that she loves her, though her mother begs her to do so. Amanda of *The Turquoise Mask* explicitly rejects her grandfather's offer to make her heiress to the fabulous family business. Others make an inheritance a national monument (*Nun's Castle*), recover memory and are blissful at no longer having to be the rich owner of a Spanish villa but only an "unemployed schoolteacher" (*Stranger in the Mirror*), and so on. If the heroines' interests can be said to be selfish in any way, it is only in their search for identity (*Cry Witch, The Golden Unicorn*), and that identity, as well, is ultimately given into their husbands' keeping.

So what was the quest all about? What was lost, forgotten, endangered, taken away? Clearly these young women have not left "empty" jobs and apartments, experienced paralyzing fear, and fled around the world, with the intention of finding themselves another "place." No, it is the escape into space that preoccupies them, the space of their own mysterious sensations, hungers, rages, and the mysterious anguish and passion they have projected onto others: Hostile or suffocating mother, passionate shadow self, and suffering child self, these are the objects of this new heroine's quest. Yet once found, these dangerous discoveries must be explicitly *dis*-owned, rejected, or pacified. In the story itself, the greed and aggression against the pre-oedipal mother and the men who replace her is released and the dark side of the mind is allowed to surface, in all its paranoia and self-loathing. But only temporarily: By story's end all that rage must go under again, be killed off, or be defined as crazy.

At this point, the rage itself deserves emphasis. In order to release rage, one must be willing to stand alone, as the bad mother and as men can do. If we have seen any consistent pattern of behavior in these heroines other than their desire for space, it is their equal and opposite fear of rupturing any human relationship. Denied, threatened, assaulted, manipulated, deceived, the heroines of these stories become "hurt," not angry.[244] They suffer physically as well as emotionally in their own bodies and in the proxy flesh of threatened children or half-crazy old women. They suffer, and then allow their "hurt" to be kissed away, like "good" girls, whose mothers are always right there to hear and soothe the tears.

A child left alone enough will pick herself up, maybe kick at the stone that tripped her, go on with the independent play that is so essential a developmental stage. It is in the early months of the second year of life that a baby begins to try to get away, to escape into a space that does not include mother; to individuate, to evolve skills of "perception, memory, cognition, reality testing."[245] If the child is a girl, her mother's response may be "stay by me, for you are like me. You need not see the world or yourself clearly or realistically; you had better not remember the important things that happen to you ; you do not need to think for yourself because others will do it for you."

If individuation is incomplete, so will separation be, and the child who has lost her self in that of her mother will never recognize either her own or her mother's self; for they have no complete selves, and what *is* there is the target (because it is inextricably like Mother) of terror and rage. The ultimate secret in the story of romantic suspense remains who is who, and what he or she is worth. We have seen these heroines attempt to solve it, to extricate themselves from the image of mother, fleeing through the emptiness of an inner world that provides no developed image of the self. We have seen them travel into the foreign countries of their unacknowledged greed and rage and terror, to the verge of self-discovery.

That remains the last secret, acknowledged briefly in the multiple deaths and dangers of these stories—briefly, and then disavowed again, so the reader can go out and buy another one to devour greedily in a continuing search for escape.

The Texts

Page numbers of important references to these texts, as they appear in sequence in this chapter, follow each bibliographical citation.

Aiken, Joan. *Castle Barebane*. New York: Viking, 1976. (175)

———. *The Silence of Herondale*. New York: Ace, 1964.

Berckman, Evelyn. *Lament for Four Brides*. New York: Dodd, Mead and Co., 1959. New York: Signet, 1974.

Berridge, Elizabeth. *Across the Common*. New York: Coward-McCann, Inc., 1964. New York: Lancer, 1966. (109, 168, 62–63, 130)

Blackmore, Jane. *Night of the Bonfire*. New York: Ace, 1974. (48, 155)

Cardiff, Sara. *The Severing Line*. New York: Random House, 1974. New York: Fawcett Crest, 1975. (206, 10)

Daniels, Dorothy. *Dark Island*. New York: Warner Books, 1972. (182–184)

———. *Illusion at Haven's Edge*. New York: Pocket Books, 1975. (69–70, 6–7)

Eden, Dorothy. *The Daughters of Ardmore Hall*. New York: Ace, 1967. (274)

———. *The Voice of the Dolls*. London: Macdonald and Co., Ltd., 1950. New York: Ace, 1977. (247, 35, 205)

Eliot, Anne. *Shadows Waiting*. New York: Hawthorn Books, Inc., 1969. Dell, 1971.

Farr, Caroline. *Mansion of Evil*. Sydney, Australia: Horwitz Publications Inc., Pty. Ltd., 1966. Signet, 1966. (221)

Gaskin, Catherine. *Edge of Glass*. Garden City, New York: Doubleday, 1967. (40)

Hintze, Naomi A. *Cry Witch*. New York: Random House, 1975. New York: Bantam, 1976. (25, 1)

Hodge, Jane Aiken. *One Way to Venice*. New York: Coward, McCann and Geoghegan, Inc., 1975. Fawcett Crest, 1976. (142)

———. *Master of Penrose* (As *Here Comes a Candle*). Garden City, New York: Doubleday, 1967. Dell, 1972. (122)

Holt, Victoria. *The Secret Woman*. Garden City, New York: Doubleday, 1970. New York: Fawcett Crest, 1971. (11, 348–349, 9, 21)

Howatch, Susan. *Call in the Night*. Briarcliff Manor, New York: Stein and Day, 1967. New York: Fawcett Crest, 1975. (136–140)

Land, Jane. *The Stranger in the Mirror.* New York: Ballentine, 1974. (3)

Melville, Jennie. *Nun's Castle.* New York: David McKay Co., Inc., 1973. New York: Fawcett Crest, 1975. (204, 87, 220, 52)

O'Brien, Saliee. *Night of the Scorpion.* New York: Medallion, 1976. (124, 206, 218, 33–34, 219)

Pilcher, Rosamunde. *Sleeping Tiger.* New York: St. Martin's Press, 1967. New York: Ballentine, 1975. (66, 8)

Scott, Genevieve. *The Water Horse.* New York: Avon, 1973. (15, 30–35)

St. Clair, Elizabeth. *Mansion in Miniature.* New York: Signet, 1977. (127, 44, 163, 147, 172, 93–99)

———. *Secret of the Locket.* New York: Signet, 1975. (7–8)

Summerton, Margaret. *Quin's Hide.* New York: E.P. Dutton and Co., 1964. New York: Ace, 1966. (7, 161, 142, 276, 283)

———. *The Sea House.* New York: Holt, Rinehart and Winston, 1960. New York: Ace, n.d. (207, 92, 210, 220, 17, 222)

Travis, Gretchen. *The Cottage.* New York: G.P. Putnam's Sons, 1973. New York: Dell, 1974.

Whitney, Phyllis. *Columbella.* Garden City, New York: Doubleday, 1966. New York: Fawcett Crest, 1967. (180, 8–9, 39, 134, 161–166)

———. *Hunter's Green.* Garden City, New York: Doubleday, 1968. New York: Fawcett, 1968. (150–151)

———. *The Golden Unicorn.* Garden City, New York: Doubleday, 1976. New York: Fawcett Crest, 1976. (10–11, 258, 87, 224–225)

———. *The Moonflower.* New York: Hawthorn Books, 1958. New York: Fawcett Crest, 1972. (12, 216)

———. *The Turquoise Mask.* Garden City, New York: Doubleday, 1974. New York: Fawcett Crest, 1978. (3)

Winston, Daoma. *A Visit After Dark.* New York: Ace, 1975. (12, 120–121)

6

THE TWO WORLDS

I. The Problem

Popular women's fiction belongs to an era in which the concept of motherhood has been, always, problematical and in need of definition and redefinition. On the evidence of our American fiction, the problem has been such that growing up to be a mother has been each heroine's only alternative, and yet a dangerous, frightening, and difficult task. The books define and redefine this task without ever suggesting a significant restructuring of roles for women, nor any actual escape from them.[246] They seem to take for granted things as they are. Beneath a surface of stereotyped characters and plot formulas and "happy endings," they reveal another sort of attachment to the status quo. These stories, from early to late, are about the fear of doing without, of being without, one exclusive love, and about the anger that accompanies this fear. In these stories, possibility after possibility is sacrificed, to prevent the realization of that deep fear. Philip Slater has called the personality that experiences these emotions "steep gradient" and explains the type by its "domination by a single nurturer,"[247] the mother of the modern nuclear family.

I have traced the terror and rage reflected in women's fiction to its origins in the girl child's inability to fully relinquish her unintegrated fantasy images of her earliest love, her mother. Unable to accept the loss of the "good" mother, she searches endlessly to project her image onto another, and to recreate it in herself. Unable to believe that she can separate from the "bad" mother, she tries endlessly to propitiate or make reparation to projections of this image. Heroine after heroine, first seduced and abandoned, then domesticated, finally believing in romantic love, has avoided growing up by a retreat into madness or self-abnegation or trivia or flirtation with death.

The fictional form dictates their psychic dis-integration into the characters in the story, good and bad, idealization and shadow. Unfortunately, such projection of the parts of the self is not merely a fictional convention. It has also been the experience of women in the historical period in question. Mother, Daughter, Home—these realities of the inner and outer worlds between 1780 and 1980 have fragmented, coalesced, fragmented again. Women have continued to lose themselves in their relationships with others.

II. The Early National Period

In the early national period, American women wrote and read books modeled on European fiction which had grown out of similar social conditions. These books depicted the anxieties produced by the modern family in its early form, and described, in the extreme sentimental gothic style, mothers who were cut off from the public sphere of experience and yet were held responsible for the protection and proper rearing of their daughters. Only these mothers had power to legitimate their daughter's safe futures—and typically they failed to do so. The daughters in these stories escaped the family roof only to punish themselves with terrors of reprisal, with insanity, and early death. Wicked mothers and men, in alliance, persecuted these young women through volumes of adventures, under other roofs, in dungeons and underground tunnels and deserted cottages, as each desperate heroine tried to find a protector she could trust.

III. The Later 19th Century

In the middle decades of the 19th century, popular women's fiction still portrayed the deficient mother. Yet here, in the genre of domestic fiction, this anxiety was masked by the Victorian fixation on an idealized maternal image. Here, the power mothers have over daughters in modern families was augmented by a religious dimension. Mothers were saviors, and in this light their restriction to the private sphere was treated as an elevation. The home was a small model of heaven, and keeping house an act of devotion. Yet the power of mothers still presented their daughters with a problem. In domestic fiction it was not solved by escape, but by the device of role-reversal. In story after story, an idealized daughter *took over as mother*. These stories attempted some integration of images, for the mothers were portrayed as deficient but still lovable. The daughters showed a concern for them (and for other family members) which was a more complex emotion than the abject helplessness of the early sentimental gothic heroines. Indeed, these mid-century heroines showed no overt aggression whatsoever against their mothers. Even maternal death in these books was not the fantasy of annihilation which it appears to have been in the earlier romances. It symbolized, rather, a further dimension of maternal power at mid-century, for a mother's influence *in memory*, from beyond the grave, was greater, if anything, than it was before her death. Her daughters accepted this dominance as readily as they assumed their role as her protector; in this configuration, they become mother, through identification with her idealized image.

In these later 19th century books, too, we notice for the first time a redefinition of fatherhood. More conspicuous by his absence than in the stories from the early national period, he was also portrayed as setting a high value indeed on traditional motherhood, in both its domestic and religious dimensions. This group of heroines were able to survive being away from home, but only temporarily, since they lacked an image of self that could support their attempts at independence. The only good men, whether fathers or potential husbands, were themselves eager to cling to the idealized mother—in the person of the heroine. So marriage with love still meant, in these stories as in the earlier ones, the recreation of a parent/child bond: The women played the child, while at the same time mothering their husbands.

This complex of mutual emotional responsibilities was even better described in the domestic fiction. Here, too, marriage *without* love drove the bride insane, although the deeper cause of her insanity was the same as in the earlier stories: She had been abandoned. Other new fictional devices seem to give evidence of a richer emotional life for the women of this period. The domestic novelists did not, indeed, make use of the classic gothic theme of the mysterious house as symbol of the female body, but they invented the theme of the apparent reincarnation, in the heroine, of her mother (the theme of the redeemed shadow) and gave a new dimension to threatened incest as a symbol of broken family ties.[248]

IV. Into the 20th Century

In the last three decades of the 19th century, and in the first three of the 20th, a house remained the place a woman was supposed to be, although now it had to be her own and not her old-fashioned mother's. This transition, so difficult for the heroines of the 19th century, is eagerly anticipated by the heroines of a newly urbanized and sophisticated America: To be *unlike* Mother is the new imperative. Of equal importance, while the heroine of mid-19th century learned neither mature sexuality nor real competence in the world outside the home, both these tasks were enjoined on fictional young women of the 20th century, with even less help from fathers than earlier heroines had had.[249]

Though fearing dependency on men as deeply as the 19th century heroine, like her, the 20th century heroine accepted it at last. The symbiotic marriage was less a seamless transfer of dependency with Mother's blessing, however, than an escape away from her into a new worldly experience. Deep defenses against a maternal image which can no longer be idealized keep these heroines involved with the "bad" mother image, in a new and complicated way. The Jungian analysis of the position is the most helpful; an entirely integrated personality will have "worked through" the contrasexual image, by realizing in herself its characteristics and values. In the 19th century this process was almost completely inhibited in many middle-class women, but at that time their role was at least defined with relative internal consistency. This is not true for women in the 20th century. Since at least the 1920s, if a girl child's mother has never tried out any aspects of the masculine image for herself, she is likely to project onto her daughter her own sense of incompetence and a deadening message of inferiority, together with a need to overcompensate for it.

Heroines of the early decades of the 20th century were regularly portrayed as under the dominance of this negative animus. Moreover, these heroines were prey to a sense of themselves as sexually unattractive. This condition of arrested adolescent narcissism (their mothers taught them) only a man could cure. Only a husband could validate a woman's attractiveness, and her *true* competence—as wife and mother.

At the same time that these internal dynamics defined a woman's limits for her, the larger culture conveyed a message that confirmed this definition. Although women were to "do" more, the essential fact about them was what they were, and where they were—at home. There was no escape from the dominance of the negative animus, especially in a society where normality, ability, and desirability were increasingly defined by the abstract authority of professionals and advertisers.[250] Ironically, a gap opened here in the lives of American women, between the images of Mother, Daughter, and Home in the dominant cultural media, and their neat congruity with images drawn from early childhood fantasy. It was ostensibly filled by a new number of available life "choices" available to women,[251] but by the middle of the 20th century its emptiness was recognized.

V. The Later 20th Century

The move to suburbia in the 1950s made this gap obvious for many women. The depersonalized heroines of romantic suspense fiction, many of whom have lost their memory of *who they are*, further dramatize what Friedan called "the problem that has no name." Their problem is that they can neither be just like mother, nor sufficiently unlike her. The confusion is social in origin, of the outer world—but the fiction continues to depict fantastic resolutions. The dis-integrated self, in which a part is dominated by another part, "frees" itself by a fictional death, a fictional marriage. The themes of inhibited or undefined woman's skill and of inhibited or undefined woman's sexuality are further developed in a greater complexity of imagery. Broken toys, illness and accidents, old pictures, masks, food, treasure, disguise and doubling, all contribute to a characterization of the "new gothic" heroine as virtually egoless, she has so much else on her mind. Not only is she more childlike (and prone to identify with children, as we have seen) and less trusting than heroines have been for a century, she is also convinced that she will never be as sexually desirable as her mother.[252]

She has, like every heroine of popular fiction, suffered a loss with which she cannot come to terms.[253] So she commences a journey which she expects will explain her inner emptiness, reveal to her the secrets of that inner world, with its gloomier attics and stranger cellars than a man's world. Identity, according to our models, depends on the internalization of figures that combine love and authority.[254] As we have seen, a resolution of such opposites is not portrayed in popular women's fiction, where primitive emotion, rather than value, is the tenor of symbol and imagery. Yet the quest—for truth, for justice—of the heroine of contemporary romance may be seen as a search for such figures of love and authority. One reason the search fails is that actual figures of authority seem no longer available.[255] The fiction therefore transposes pre-oedipal superego and negative animus onto an authority substitute, the "new" strong hero. The quest, then, while it is an attempt to rid the house of mysterious evil, is also an attempt to fill it with goodness, with a "normal family," as defined by infantile wishes, television, and the experts.

VI. Choosing Worlds

In real life, the people to whom we are related by necessity or desire often receive, as the Jungians say, the projections of our inner world. In real life, we cannot usually kill them because they are bad; in real life, a marriage does not symbolize the union of fully developed opposites that precedes individuation.[256] Yet outside romantic fiction we can learn to recognize and repossess those projections, to occupy the house of the self with knowledge of ourselves and consequently of others, whom we then can see clearly. Gilbert and Gubar speak of the difference between fictional "necromancy," as an art of resurrection, and "image magic," which is the self-punishing capitulation to conventional social roles and to the static fantasies of our inner world.[257] The heroines of contemporary romance do resurrect their anger and their hunger—but not for long. Like all heroines of popular romance, they are unable to integrate them.

The great majority of Americans in 1980 are still marrying and having children, and they are still doing so without basic restructuring of the family.[258] In our lifetimes, popular women's fiction in America will continue to reflect the ambivalences of women whose infancy has given them a "steep gradient" personality,[259] and whose subsequent relations with occupational and consumption roles will exacerbate rather than relieve insecurity. The family is likely to continue to function as affirmation of our own human reality, in a time that seems to have overwhelmed the moral capacities of fathers and mothers, and the faith that our children will be better. We are not, probably, going to become less dependent on each other, even if we are able to invent and implement new forms of nurturance and support. The central paradox of the modern family is that it creates and encourages a desire for individual autonomy by providing a context where it may be, and sometimes has to be, given up. This paradox, and the constants in human need that have shaped the materials that are the subject of this book, must be understood, must be imagined and re-imagined in the years to come.

Nineteenth century domestic fiction, as I have mentioned, existed side by side with the work of feminists who were able to imagine woman's independent strength, and feminists were still doing so throughout the Progressive Era. In the 1960s and 1970s, women have received more positive attention from other women than in nearly half a century before, as feminists have looked for new images of love and authority.[260] These are beginnings. We must deliberately and consciously accept, for the present, the social and psychological facts of our dis-integration. We have not yet defined what a mother is, or a daughter, or even a woman. We are not even sure what we want these words to mean, and this has been the case with American women for at least two centuries. We are not living, now, through a historical moment of unique crisis, yet we are now developing unique materials and skills for meeting crises. We need not accept entirely any idea of "normal" development or being, whether object–relations theory, Jungian theory, the work of feminist therapists, or literary critics. Each may have its use in revealing us to ourselves. If we learn to outgrow the power of the maternal archetype to fill us with terror or impossible longing, then perhaps we may learn to understand that power as our own strength. That is not a fictional quest; it will eventually take us outside ourselves.

Chapter One

[1]Nancy F. Cott, *The Bonds of Womanhood: "Woman's Sphere" in New England, 1780–1835* (New Haven, Connecticut: Yale Univ. Press, 1977) provides in her conclusion an excellent summary of scholarly evaluations and re-evaluations of woman's position in America in the 19th century, as based on just such an arbitrary distinction among source materials.

[2]See Marjorie Fiske and Leo Lowenthal, The debate over art and popular culture: Eighteenth century England as a case study, in *Literature, Popular Culture and Society*, ed. Leo Lowenthal, (New York: Prentice-Hall, 1961) for a description of the genesis and eventual acceptance of popular fiction.

[3]Sheila Rowbotham, *Hidden From History: Three Hundred Years of Women's Oppression and the Fight Against It* (London: Pluto Press, 1973), p. 9, and Lawrence Stone, *The Family, Sex and Marriage in England 1500–1800* (London: Weidenfeld and Nicolson, 1977), pp. 656, 661. Carl Degler, *At Odds: Women and the Family in America from the Revolution to the Present* (New York: Oxford Univ. Press, 1980), supports this view.

[4]Peter Gregg Slater, *Views of Children and of Child Rearing During the Early National Period* (Ann Arbor: University Microfilms, 1970), pp. 165–166.

[5]Rowbotham, p. 3. See also Elise Boulding, *The Underside of History* (Boulder, Colorado: Westview Press, 1976), Ch. 10.

[6]Though Edward Shorter, in *The Making of the Modern Family* (New York: Basic Books, 1975), p. 199, claims that America was "born modern."

[7]Cott, pp. 8 and 24; and also Patricia Branca, Image and reality: The myth of the ideal Victorian woman, in *Clio's Consciousness Raised: New Perspectives on the History of Women* (New York: Harper and Row, 1974).

[8]John Cawelti, *Adventure, Mystery and Romance: Formula Stories* (Chicago: Univ. of Chicago Press, 1976), defines a literary formula as "a structure of narrative or dramatic conventions employed in a great number of individual works," and further specifies that it may involve a conventional way of treating a thing or person, p. 5.

[9]Mark Poster, *Critical Theory of the Family* (New York: The Seabury Press, 1980), p. 141. "Industrial capitalism and representative democracy, for example, do not emerge at the same time as modern family forms."

[10]Kenneth Keniston, Psychological development and historical change, in *The Family in History*, eds. Theodore K. Rabb and Robert I. Rotberg (New York: Octagon Books, 1976), comments that some societies "may 'create' stages of life that

do not exist in other societies; some societies may 'stop' human development in some sectors far earlier than other societies 'choose' to do so," p. 154. While no one who has written on 19th century women's fiction has entirely missed the point that it tends to have, as its "secret message," "the story of the woman's quest for self-definition" (Sandra M. Gilbert and Susan Gubar, *The Madwoman in the Attic: The Woman Writer and the Nineteenth Century Literary Imagination* [New Haven: Yale Univ. Press, 1979], p. 76, and see also Nina Baym, *Woman's Fiction: A Guide to Novels by and about Women in America, 1820–1870* [Ithaca: Cornell Univ. Press, 1978], p. 19 and Ch. 2), our society has not yet stopped stopping human development in some sectors.

[11] As Roberta Hamilton points out, "The fundamental changes in the family [and hence in women's roles] occur . . . not with industrialization but with capitalism." *The Liberation of Women: A Study of Patriarchy and Capitalism* (London: George Allen and Unwin, 1978), p. 18. Summary statements of this earlier change in psychic structure (i.e., the sexual division into private and public spheres) are to be found in Stone, Chs. 7 and 13. He also discusses New England families. For discussion of Mother's changing role see Shorter, and of Father's (chiefly the effects of his increasing absence from the home) see Peter Laslett, *Family Life and Illicit Love in Earlier Generations* (Cambridge: Cambridge University Press, 1977), p. 37.

[12] Juliet Mitchell, *Psychoanalysis and Feminism* (New York: Random House, 1974), pp. 374 ff.; Gayle Rubin, The traffic in women: Notes of the "political economy of sex," in *Toward an Anthropology of Women*, ed. Rayna R. Reiter (New York: Monthly Review Press, 1975), pp. 185, 193.

[13] Miriam M. Johnson, Heterosexuality, the father and male dominance, available from the Center for the Sociological Study of Women, University of Oregon, Eugene, Oregon 97403.

[14] M. D. Faber, in an excellent essay, Analytic prolegomena to the study of western tragedy, *Hartford Studies in Literature* 5 (1973), p. 54, discusses the situation as it has always obtained within Western culture. "A mother-dominated home in a patriarchal society is 'destined' to catalyze maturational problems . . . ." A capitalist–industrial society has merely made them more inevitable.

[15] Baym, op. cit.; Herbert Ross Brown, *The Sentimental Novel in America 1789–1860* (New York: Pageant Books, 1959); Helen Waite Papashvily, *All the Happy Endings: A Study of the Domestic Novel in America, the Women Who Wrote It, the Women Who Read It, in the Nineteenth Century* (New York: Harper, 1956); Montague Summers, *The Gothic Quest: A History of the Gothic Novel* (London: Fortune Press, 1968); J.M.S. Tompkins, *The Popular Novel in England 1770–1800* (London: Constable and Co., 1932), relate especially to the purposes of this study.

[16] Rubin, p. 159; Mitchell *passim*. See also Annis Pratt, Archetypal approaches to the new feminist criticism, *Bucknell Review* 21 (Spring 1973): *passim*.

[17] I refer here to the efforts of the "Buffalo School" of criticism, in particular the recent work of Norman O. Holland.

[18]Clifton Snider, Jung's theory of the archetype and creativity (Part I), *Psychocultural Review* (Winter 1977), p. 98.

[19]C.G. Jung, *Modern Man in Search of a Soul* (New York: Harcourt, Brace, 1933), p. 178.

[20]An overview of Klein and Fairbairn is provided in Harry Guntrip, *Personality Structure and Human Interaction* (New York: Basic Books, 1961). D.S. Winnicott's *Playing and Reality* (New York: Basic Books, 1971) is most relevant to our purposes. More recently, two American women, Dorothy Dinnerstein, in *The Mermaid and the Minotaur* (New York: Harper, 1976) and Nancy Friday, *My Mother, Myself* (New York: Dell, 1977) have attempted to popularize some elements of this perspective.

[21]Margaret S. Mahler, Fred Pine and Anni Bergman, *The Psychological Birth of the Human Infant* (New York: Basic Books, 1975), p. 48. See also Otto Kernberg, Early ego integration and object relations, *Annals of the New York Academy of Sciences* (1972) for a detailed outline of the process.

[22]James F. Masterson and Donald B. Rinsley, The borderline syndrome: The role of the mother in the genesis and psychic structure of the borderline personality, *International Journal of Psychoanalysis* 56 (1975): 169.

[23]Although Jung does not ignore the importance of such early experiences. On the contrary, he explains that differentiation from the Self archetypes of wise old man or great mother, for example, are "for the man, the second and real liberation from the father, and, for the woman, liberation from the mother. . . ." *Two Essays on Analytical Psychology* (Princeton, New Jersey: Princeton Univ. Press, 1966), p. 235. Also it should be noted here that neo-Freudian Erik H. Erikson has written at length on the developmental tasks of *each* stage of human life. See his Identity and the life cycle, *Psychological Issues* 1, Monograph #1, 1959.

[24]Jung, *Two Essays*, p. 151.

[25]Jung, *Two Essays*, p. 96.

[26]Klein's position here is derived from her version of Freud's "biological mysticism of Eros and Thanatos," Harry Guntrip, *Psychoanalytic Theory, Therapy, and the Self* (New York: Basic Books, 1973), p. 55.

[27]Dr. Carlos Estrada, class in Normal Personality Development, Menninger School of Psychiatry, Autumn, 1977.

[28]For a detailed discussion and some evidence for these ideas, see Melanie Klein and Joan Riviere, *Love, Hate and Reparation* (London: Hogarth Press, 1937); Janine Chasseguet-Smirgel, Freud and female sexuality, *International Journal of Psychoanalysis* (1976); Joseph Rheingold, *The Mother, Anxiety and Death* (Boston: Little, Brown, 1967).

[29]Simon O. Lesser, in his unsurpassed *Fiction and the Unconscious* (New York: Random House, 1957), p. 200, describes the sort of response to fiction that I mean: "we compose stories structured upon the ones we read (or upon parts of them) which

give us an opportunity to relive or alter our actual experience or act out dramas revolving around our wishes and fears."

[30]Patrick Bratlinger, Romance, novels and psychoanalysis, in *The Practice of Psychoanalytic Criticism*, ed. Leonard Tennenhouse (Detroit, Michigan: Wayne State Univ. Press, 1976), p. 25.

[31]For example, Richard Chase, *The American Novel and its Tradition* (Garden City, New York: Doubleday, 1957), pp. 12–13; and Northrup Frye, *The Anatomy of Criticism* (Princeton, New Jersey: Princeton Univ. Press, 1957), pp. 187, 193 and 198–200 in particular.

[32]Bratlinger, p. 37.

[33]Chase, p. 12.

[34]Wolfgang Iser, *The Implied Reader: Patterns of Communication in Prose Fiction from Bunyan to Beckett* (Baltimore, Maryland: Johns Hopkins, 1974), p. 283.

[35]Iser, p. 291.

[36]Freud, in his 1919 essay, The uncanny, in Vol. 17 of *The Standard Edition of the Complete Psychoanalytical Work of Sigmund Freud* translated under the editorship of James Strachey, with Anna Freud, Alix Strachey, and Alan Tyson (London: Hogarth Press, 1953–), p. 252, speaks of the sense that this material should have remained secret and hidden—his examples run an extremely relevant gamut from talking dolls, through doubles, family curses, and live burial to "factors of silence, solitude and darkness... actually elements in the production of the infantile anxiety from which the majority of human beings have never become quite free."

[37]In addition to the Jungian and object–relations view, see Otto Rank's psychoanalytic study, *The Double*, translated and ed. Harry Tucker, Jr. (Chapel Hill, North Carolina: University of North Carolina Press, 1971), and Robert Rogers, *A Psychoanalytic Study of the Double in Literature* (Detroit, Michigan: Wayne State Univ. Press, 1970). The "not-me" is a part of Harry Stack Sullivan's typology. See *The Interpersonal Theory of Psychiatry* (New York: Norton, 1953). The concept is also brilliantly discussed in Marion Milner, Aspects of symbolism in comprehension of the not-self, *International Journal of Psychoanalysis* 33 (1952), where her concern is to show that the symbol has integrative as well as defensive functions.

[38]So that we cannot use to its limits the suggestion that characters be treated the subjects of clinical case histories, as put forth by Frederick Crews, *Out of My System: Psychoanalysis, Ideology, and Critical Method* (New York: Oxford Univ. Press, 1975), p. 15, and W.W. Meissner, Some notes on the psychology of the literary character: A psychoanalytic perspective, *Seminars in Psychiatry* 5 (1973), especially pp. 266–267, where he discusses fiction as resembling Winnicott's "potential space."

[39]R.A. Spitz, *The First Year of Life* (New York: International Universities Press, 1965); John Bowlby, Grief and mourning in infancy and early childhood, *The Psychoanalytic Study of the Child* (1960). This is also Klein's view.

[40]Gilbert and Gubar, p. 79, "There is a sense, then, in which the female literary tradition ... participates on all levels in the same duality or duplicity that necessitates the generation of such doubles as monster characters who shadow angelic authors and mad anti-heroines who complicate the lives of sane heroines."

[41]Frye, pp. 186–187.

[42]Tzvetan Todorov, *The Fantastic: A Structural Approach to a Literary Genre* (Ithaca, New York: Cornell Univ. Press, 1975), p. 47, comments of the uncanny that its emotion is "uniquely linked to the sentiments of the characters and not to a material event defying reason." In other words, the supernatural elements in these books are the supernatural figures which arise from the depth of the psyche.

[43]I am in agreement with Norman O. Holland and Leona F. Sherman, Gothic possibilities, *New Literary History* 8 (1977), that these dwelling places can symbolize the mother's body. However, they symbolize the heroine's too, at times—and therefore the complexity of her relation to that female body which "gave" her her female body. See also Nancy Regan, A house of one's own: Women's bodies in recent women's fiction, *Journal of Popular Culture* II (Spring 1978): *passim*; and Kathryn Weibel, *Mirror, Mirror: Images of Women Reflected in Popular Culture* (New York: Anchor Books, 1977), p. 225.

[44]Faber, p. 51.

Chapter Two

[45]Cott, p. 4. See also Ch. 3 in Mary P. Ryan, *Womanhood in America from Colonial Times to the Present* (New York: Franklin Watts, 1975); Slater, p. 4; Daniel Scott Smith, Parental power and marriage patterns: An analysis of historical trends in Hingham, Massachusetts, *Journal of Marriage and the Family* (August 1973): 426. See also Degler, Ch. 1.

[46]Ryan, pp. 103 ff. See also Gerda Lerner, The lady and the mill girl: Changes in the status of women in the age of Jackson, in *Women and Womanhood in America*, eds. Ronald W. Hogeland and Aileen S. Kraditor (Lexington, Massachusetts: D.C. Heath, 1973), pp. 90–92.

[47]Slater, p. 176; Smith, *passim*.

[48]Linda K. Kerber, Daughters of Columbia: Educating women for the Republic, 1787–1805, *The Hofstader Aegis*, eds. Stanley Elkins and Eric McKitrick (New York: Knopf, 1974), p. 58.

[49]Barbara Sicherman, Review essay: American history, *Signs* 1 (Winter, 1975), p. 469; Ruth H. Bloch, American feminine ideals in transition: The rise of the moral mother, 1785–1815, *Feminist Studies* 4 (June 1978), p. 109; Degler, p. 73.

[50]Bloch, pp. 111–115.

[51]Monica Kiefer, *American Children Through Their Books* (Philadelphia: Univ. of Pennsylvania Press, 1948), p. 229.

[52]Cott, p. 9.

[53]The fact that deliberate limitations of family size were a part of this whole shift of emphasis is by no means irrelevant. See Daniel Scott Smith, Family limitation, sexual control and domestic feminism in Victorian America, in *A Heritage of Her Own: Toward a New Social History of American Women*, eds. Nancy Cott and Elizabeth H. Pleck (New York: Simon and Schuster, 1979).

[54]Carroll Smith-Rosenberg, The female world of love and ritual: Relations between women in nineteenth-century America, *Signs* 1 (Autumn, 1975): 9. See also Phillida Bunkle, Sentimental womanhood and domestic education, 1830–1870, *History of Education Quarterly* 14 (Spring, 1974).

[55]Stone, pp. 284–286.

[56]Mary Sumner Benson, *Women in Eighteenth Century America: A Study of Opinion and Social Usage, #405 Columbia University Studies in History, Economics and Public Law* (New York: Columbia Univ. Press, 1935), p. 79. Accurate figures are

unobtainable. See Hellmut Lehmann-Haupt, *The Book in America* (New York: R.R. Bowker Co., 1952), pp. 123–124; and Frank Mott, *Golden Multitudes* (New York: Macmillan, 1947), pp. 7–9.

[57]Papashvily, p. 25.

[58]Nina Baym, Portrayal of women in American literature, 1790–1870, in *What Manner of Women: Essays on English and American Life and Literature*, ed. Marlene Springer (New York: New York Univ. Press, 1977), p. 229.

[59]Benson, p. 188.

[60]This critical opinion is quoted in Ann Stanford, Images of women in early American literature, in Springer, p. 203. For the British tradition, see Fisk and Lowenthal; Ioan Williams, *Novel and Romance* (Boston: Routledge and Kegan Paul, 1970); and John Tennon Taylor, *Early Opposition to the English Novel* (New York: King's Crown Press, 1943).

[61]Kerber, p. 38.

[62]William Charvat, *The Origins of American Critical Thought 1810–1835* (New York: A.S. Barnes and Co., 1961), p. 138.

[63]Benson, p. 191.

[64]Cott, pp. 167–168. "To identify women with the heart was to imply that they conducted themselves through life by engaging the affections of others. The cultural metonymy by which the nurturant maternal role stood for the whole of women's experience further confirmed that 'heartfelt' caring was women's characteristic virtue."

[65]Barbara Welter, The cult of true womanhood: 1820–1860, *American Quarterly*, 18 (Summer, 1966).

[66]Ernest Earnest, *The American Eve in Fact and Fiction, 1775–1914* (Urbana: Univ. of Illinois Press, 1974), p. 47, quotes both Tocqueville and Mrs. Trollope on the obviousness of this change of status.

[67]John J. Richetti, *Popular Fiction Before Richardson* (New York: Oxford Univ. Press, 1969) describes these romances. My favorite example of them, popular in America, is Penelope Aubin's *Noble Slaves*, in which one heroine acts quickly to prevent her rape by a Turk—she tears out her eyes and throws them at him. He desists.

[68]Bridget G. MacCarthy, *The Later Women Novelists: 1744–1818* (New York: William Sallock, 1948), pp. 45–46.

[69]*The Cyclo Paedia of American Literature*, Vol. I, Evert A. and George L. Duyckinck (Philadelphia: William Rutter and Co., 1877), p. 521.

[70]Kernberg, pp. 234–237.

[71]Hanna Segal, *Introduction to the Work of Melanie Klein* (New York: Basic Books, 1973), p. 25.

[72]Ryan, pp. 133–134.

[73]Segal, p. 27.

[74]Slater, pp. 176–177. See also Anne Scott MacLeod, A Moral Tale: Children's Fiction and American Culture 1820–1860 (Hamden, England: Archon, 1975), pp. 73–77.

[75]M. Esther Harding, The Parental Image: Its Injury and Reconstruction: A Study in Analytic Psychology (New York: Putnams, 1965), p. 11.

[76]Harding, p. 8, describes the difficulties of separating from a possessive mother. In these books, there is no other kind.

[77]Harding, p. 102, speaks of such substitutes as providing the opportunity to outgrow dependence.

[78]MacCarthy, p. 153.

[79]The novel, like The Coquette, is based on a historical case.

[80]See, for example, Walter E. Houghton, The Victorian Frame of Mind, 1830–1870 (New Haven: Yale Univ. Press, 1957), Ch. 13.

[81]Harding, p. 15.

[82]Nina Baym, Women's Fiction, pp. 25–26.

[83]Doris Mary Stenton, The English Woman in History (London: Unwin, 1957), p. 299.

[84]Klein and Riviere, p. 68.

[85]Cott, pp. 36–37. 40.

[86]See Holland and Sherman, p. 283. See also Gilbert and Gubar, pp. 87ff.

[87]The hero of Montalbert, whose mother controls the money and hence his inclinations, feels shock at the thought of what a release for him her death would be: "she alone was the barrier between him and his happiness," p. 267. The daughters in these stories do not have such thoughts to shock themselves with.

[88]Cott, p. 32. "As family centered production gave ground to market-oriented production and individual wage earning, school teaching became a more important financial resource for young women."

[89]Cott, p. 21.

[90]Klein and Riviere, p. 7. "In a stable political and economic system there is a great deal of apparent liberty and opportunity to fulfill our own needs, and we do not as a rule feel our dependence on the organization in which we live." This study begins and ends in periods of instability.

Chapter Three

[91]Degler's view of this "Cult of True Womanhood" is that, while it circumscribed women's activities, it also represented an advance in their status. It resulted in material improvements in their condition, and also assigned them the role of companions or even superiors to men, pp. 27–28. There are some problems here which I hope to clarify in the following chapter. Degler, in his later chapters, documents 19th century American woman's protection of the home from "the world's evil" by social action. There is no doubt that the doctrine of her "divine influence" had such practical consequences. In fiction, however, we are presented with another picture.

[92]Ryan, pp. 141–143.

[93]Papashvily, p. 35.

[94]Amaury de Riencourt, *Sex and Power in History* (New York: David McKay, 1974), p. 312. Southworth's novels, often set in England or the antebellum American South, are sometimes an exception.

[95]Ann Douglas, *The Feminization of American Culture* (New York: Alfred A. Knopf, 1977), p. 62; Ryan, pp. 147–148; Smith-Rosenberg, p. 133.

[96]MacLeod, pp. 31 ff.

[97]Hale, Parton, McIntosh, Southworth, Hentz, Warner, Stephens, and Evans.

[98]Ann Douglas, The "scribbling women" and Fanny Fern: Why women wrote, *American Quarterly* 23 (Spring 1971): 5–12, documents this delicacy. Baym also comments on it, and its passing.

[99]Baym remarks that they saw their work as a *job* rather than *art*. Gilbert and Gubar's best comment on the literary tradition in question is that "foremothers... have both overtly and covertly conveyed their traditional anxiety of authorship to their bewildered female descendents," p. 54.

[100]Douglas, *The Feminization of American Culture*, p. 63; MacLeod, *passim*; and Bernard Wishy, *The Child and the Republic: The Dawn of Modern American Child Nurture* (Philadelphia: Univ. of Pennsylvania Press, 1968), *passim*; Joseph F. Kett, *Rites of Passage: Adolescence in America 1790 to the Present* (New York: Basic Books, 1977), pp. 75–79. Sara Delamont, The domestic ideology in women's education, in *The Nineteenth Century Woman: Her Cultural and Physical World* (New York: Barnes and Noble, 1978), eds. Sara Delamont and Lorna Duffin, p. 164. Degler, pp. 308–311, describes the movement for equal *education* of boys and girls at this time, mentioning that it fits in easily with the idea of women as child rearers and companions to men, and that it stopped short at the college level.

[101]Joseph F. Kett, Adolescence and youth in nineteenth century America, in *The Family in History*, eds. Theodore Rabb and Robert I. Rothberg (New York: Octagon Books, 1976), p. 107, indicates that girls were seen as having a particularly dangerous and difficult passage into adulthood. See also Lorna Duffin, The conspicuous consumptive: Woman as invalid, in Delamont and Duffin, pp. 32–38.

[102]Baym, p. 35.

[103]MacLeod, p. 129, mentions that even in children's fiction they were being criticized for neglecting families while pursuing success–this at the same time they were portrayed regularly as failures as providers! Degler mentions the "relatively democratic role of the father" along with his absence as reasons for mothers' new significance, p. 77.

[104]As Baym, p. 25, suggests.

[105]Papashvily grounds this revenge motive in the writers' real-life experience of betrayal. I do not know that such experience makes of these writers an exceptional group.

[106]Peter Gregg Slater, *Children in the New England Mind, in Death and Life* (New York: Archon Books, 1977), p. 141.

[107]Slater, p. 149.

[108]An excellent description of this state (or absence) of mind in Peter T. Cominos, The innocent *femina sensualis* in unconscious conflict, in Martha Vicinus, ed., *Suffer and Be Still: Women in the Victorian Age* (Bloomington, Indiana: Indiana Univ. Press, 1972). His topic is Victorian England. Ben Barker-Benfield, The spermatic economy: A nineteenth century view of sexuality, in *The American Family in Social–Historical Perspective*, ed. Michael Gordon (New York: St. Martin's Press, 1973), describes how American economic man's imagined need to keep his sexual capital in the bank, so to speak, was projected onto women in the form of her repression, representing "social order generally," p. 349. Nancy F. Cott gives another view: that women themselves assumed this repression as a not-very-successful way of rescuing themselves from sexual vulnerability and exploitation, Passionlessness: An interpretation of Victorian sexual ideology 1790–1850, *Signs* 4 (Winter 1978), 219–236.

[109]MacLeod, p. 129.

[110]Slater, p. 163.

[111]Nancy Chodorow, *The Reproduction of Mothering: Psychoanalysis and the Sociology of Gender* (Berkeley: The Univ. of California Press, 1978), p. 193.

[112]Phyllis Greenacre, *Emotional Growth*, Vol. 1 (New York: International Universities Press, 1971), p. 145.

[113]Chodorow, p. 97.

[114]Segal, pp. 68–77. See also MacLeod, pp. 73–77 for an example of this emotional condition portrayed in children's fiction of the period.

[115]I am suspicious of attempts to match up theories of individual psychological development to historical "developments." (Glenn Davis, *Childhood and History in America*, [New York: Psychohistory Press, 1976] is more persuasive than most because it is more specific and detailed than most.) Having issued this caveat, I will continue to register—specifically and in detail—my impression that the infantile fantasies surfacing in these stories at mid-19th century are less "primitive," in the psychoanalytic sense, than those in earlier fiction. It is readily observable that these stories display far greater realism, and greater complexity in both the inner and outer worlds.

[116]Chodorow, pp. 69–70.

[117]In her brief discussion of this passage, p. 71, Baym emphasizes the equivalence of father and husband for the heroine. This is of course a far less important or even interesting equation than the one between mother and daughter which underlies the utter reliability of Ruth's—and others'—tenderness and fidelity.

[118]Baym's misreading here, p. 285, is serious.

[119]The reader is reminded of the doctor's orders, based on Weir-Mitchell's "rest cure," in Charlotte Perkins Gilman's *The Yellow Wallpaper* (1892), which, obeyed, drove the sick woman mad.

[120]Degler comments that the closer a female activity was associated with the moral and domestic responsibilities of women, the more likely it was to be condoned and accepted, p. 306.

[121]Douglas, p. 92. See also Kathryn Kish Sklar, *Catharine Beecher: A Study in American Domesticity* (New York: Norton, 1976), pp. 204–205, for an excellent analysis of female invalidism: "Perhaps most importantly, invalidism was a way of marking... exclusion from the culture's dominant values of competition, achievement, strength, and self-assertion." See also Duffin.

[122]Cott, Passionlessness..., p. 234, sums up the evidence for this. See also Degler, Chs. 8–12.

[123]Barker-Benfield's point.

[124]Carroll Smith-Rosenberg and Charles Rosenberg, The female animal: Medical and biological views of woman and her role in nineteenth century America, *The Journal of American History* 59 (1973): 350–353. Women, Lasch insists, "welcomed the substitution of doctors for midwives in childbirth. The redefinition of pregnancy as a disease requiring medical intervention helped women in their campaign for voluntary motherhood." *New York Review of Books* 12 (June 1980): 27. Nevertheless, the 19th century spread of puerperal fever was a direct result of this substitution. See Richard W. Wertz and Dorothy C. Wertz, *Lying In: A History of Childbirth in America* (New York: Free Press, 1977), pp. 120–228. Gilbert and Gubar comment on the psychological connection between dying mothers and the cult of true womanhood: "To be selfless... is to be dead," p. 25.

[125]For a discussion of this phenomenon, see Donald B. Rinsley's An object–relations view of the borderline personality, in Peter Hartocullis, ed. *Borderline Personality Disorders* (New York: International Universities Press, 1977), pp. 47–70.

[126]D.W. Winnicott, The capacity to be alone, *International Journal of Psychoanalysis* 39 (Fall 1958): 416–417.

[127]Hentz herself had some stake in this attitude. See Riley, p. 222, for her experiences as educator.

[128]Marie-Louise Von Franz, The process of individuation, in *Man and His Symbols*, ed. C. G. Jung (Garden City, New York: Doubleday, 1964), p. 191.

[129]Von Franz, *Shadow and Evil in Fairytales* (Zurich: Spring Publications, 1974), pp. 172, 202.

[130]Compare Baym's definition of terms, pp. 33–35.

[131]Baym, p. 35.

[132]Klein and Riviere, pp. 27–28.

[133]Brown, p. 362.

[134]C. G. Jung, *Two Essays*, pp. 156–157. MacLeod, pp. 84–91, comments on the ambivalences of this character type as portrayed in children's literature.

[135]Chodorow, p. 75. See also Philip Slater, *Earthwalk* (New York: Bantam, 1975), pp. 130 ff.

[136]Harding, p. 151.

[137]In two of these novels, *Lucy Howard's Journal*, p. 222 and *The Hidden Path*, pp. 430–431, we hear of how deeply wrong it is for a young married couple to live in a *boarding* house!

[138]Mahler, et al., p. 44.

[139]Ryan, p. 172, comments "The contradictions of the feminine role-model were, in fact, built into the emphatic core of sentimental literature, the threatened estrangement, departure or death of loved ones." More to the point, perhaps, is her description of how children's deaths "preserved women from terrestrial separation from their young," p. 171—obviously this worked the other way, and a mother's death made her omnipresent.

[140]Mary Kelley, in The sentimentalists: Promise and betrayal in the home," *Signs* 4 (Spring 1979), suggests that the few good men in this group of books are actually studies in "the feminization of the male," p. 442. Chodorow suggests a reason for men's approval of the child wife: "Nearly exclusive maternal care . . . creates men's resentment and dread of women, and their search for non-threatening, undemanding, dependent, even infantile women," p. 185. See also Baym, pp. 290–291: "The man whose life is unblemished by acts of brutality or exploitation, who comes not as a conqueror or manipulator but as a friend and guide, is the one who catches the imagination of most of the women novelists."

[141]Chodorow, pp. 125, 140.

[142]Miriam M. Johnson, Fathers, mothers and sex typing, *Sociological Inquiry* 45 (1975), p. 16.

[143]All three of these female characters play a maternal role which is subtly terrible.

Catharine's ability to physically cripple a daughter is clearly imaged; the ability to mutilate psychologically, shared by all three, is of course the real point.

[144]The process that Ann Douglas describes in Ch. 4 of *The Feminization of American Culture* has yet to reach a final stage.

[145]As Cott, in Passionlessness..., p. 236, comments, "claims of women's moral influence [obscured]... the need for other sources of power."

[146]Luciano P. R. Santiago, *The Children of Oedipus* (Roslyn Heights, New York: Libra Publishers, 1973), p. 113.

[147]Rubin, p. 173.

[148]Rubin, p. 193.

[149]Baym, p. 298; Papashvily, pp. 180–207.

[150]Douglas says that the "feminizing" sentimental forces of the period would "generate mass culture redefined and perhaps limit... the possibilities for change in American society," p. 13. In the next chapter I illustrate this proposition, but also show that there *was* significant change in the direction of what she calls a "sexually diversified culture," in the years before World War II.

Chapter Four

[151]Gerda Lerner, *The Woman in American History* (Menlo Park, California: Addison-Wesley Publishing Company, 1971), p. 95 ff. See also Anne Firor Scott, *The Southern Lady: From Pedestal to Politics 1830–1930* (Chicago: Univ. of Chicago Press, 1970), p. 100.

[152]Jacques Donzelot, *The Policing of Families* (New York: Pantheon, 1979), pp. 52–54.

[153]Gilman M. Ostrander, The revolution in morals, in John Braeman, Robert H. Bremner and David Brody, eds., *Changes and Continuity in Twentieth Century America: The 1920s* (Columbus, Ohio: Ohio State Univ. Press, 1968), pp. 324–327; Sheila M. Rothman, *Woman's Proper Place: A History of Changing Ideals and Practices, 1870 to the Present* (New York: Basic Books, 1978), p. 13 ff.

[154]Degler, pp. 376, 383–384. In 1900, 4% of married white women worked outside the home; in 1940, still only 12%.

[155]William D. Andrews and Deborah C. Andrews, Technology and the housewife in nineteenth century America, *Women's Studies* 2 (1974): 315–316. See also Rothman, Ch. 3; Alice Kessler-Harris, Women, work and the social order, in Berenice A. Carroll, ed. *Liberating Women's History: Theoretical and Critical Essays* (Urbana, Illinois: Univ. of Illinois Press, 1976), p. 332.

[156]Degler, p. 326, paraphrasing William O'Neill in *Everyone Was Brave: The Rise and Fall of Feminism in America* (Chicago: Quadrangle, 1969).

[157]See Ch. 13. The related point, that the liberal view of the state could be saved only by a change in the ideology of the family, is also Donzelot's central thesis.

[158]Degler, pp. 357–358.

[159]Geoffrey H. Steere, Child-rearing literature and modernization theory, *The Family in Historical Perspective* (Winter, 1974), pp. 8–10.

[160]Leo Markun, in *Mrs. Grundy* (New York: D. Appleton and Company, 1930), dates the change from a much earlier period: "After the Civil War a general reaction appeared against the extreme prudery which had previously prevailed in the United States," p. 559.

[161]Degler, pp. 419 ff. See also Carol Ruth Berkin and Mary Beth Norton, *Women of America: A History* (Boston: Houghton-Mifflin Co., 1979), pp. 276–283, on the differences between the changes effected, for women, by the two World Wars.

[162]Robert H. Wiebe, *Search for Order: 1877–1920* (New York: Hill and Wang, 1967), *passim*.

[163]Berkin and Norton, p. 277.

[164]Frank Stricker, Cookbooks and law books: The hidden history of career women in twentieth-century America, in Cott and Pleck, p. 478.

[165]Degler, pp. 383–384 and 419 ff.

[166]Christopher Lasch, *Haven in a Heartless World: The Family Beseiged* (New York: Basic Books, 1977), p. 10. Also see Rothman, Chs. 3 and 4.

[167]At the end of the 1920s, a European comments, "'There goes an American . . . . The classless way they dress. Filing clerk and company president's wife. The same nylons, little hats, tweed suits, navy blue dresses.' The mass culture has done its work." Quoted in Mary Ellen Roach and Joan Bubolz Eicher, *Dress, Advancement and the Social Order* (New York: John Wiley and Sons, 1965), p. 341.

[168]Stuart Ewen, *Captains of Consciousness: Advertising and the Social Roots of the Consumer Culture* (New York: McGraw-Hill, 1976), p. 102.

[169]As Julie Roy Jeffrey, in *Frontier Woman: The Trans-Mississippi West 1840–1880* (New York: Hill and Wang, 1979) characterizes its role on the frontier, where "women valued themselves and were valued for their traditional qualities," p. 198.

[170]Writers of our period were immensely successful with these—for example, Stratton-Porter, Burnett, Wiggin, Inez Irwin (who also wrote a history of feminism), Bruckner (who wrote "nurse" books for "teens").

[171]Elaine Showalter's term for a genre of women's fiction invented in 19th century Britain. See *A Literature of Their Own: British Women Novelists from Bronte to Lessing* (Princeton, New Jersey: Princeton Univ. Press, 1977), p. 154. Examples of the genre in America in this study are the works of Downing, Downs, Ward, Libbey, Bryan, Clay, Wilcox. Elinor Glyn's books are perhaps an offshoot. Southworth's later works verge more and more in this direction (she was still being reissued in the twenties).

[172]Elaine Showalter, ed. *These Modern Women: Autobiographical Essays from the Twenties* (Old Westbury, New York: The Feminist Press, 1978), p. 13, comments that advertising doubled in volume in the 1920s, which also saw the rise of the cosmetics and fashion industries in America. "Mass production democratized clothing and cosmetics," comments June Sochen, *Movers and Shakers: American Women Thinkers and Activists, 1900–1970* (New York: Quadrangle/The New York Times Book Company, 1973), p. 101. See also the introduction to Gaye Tuchman, Arlene Kaplan Daniels and James Benet, eds. *Hearth and Home: Images of Women in the Mass Media* (New York: Oxford Univ. Press, 1978) for a theoretical perspective on such phenomena.

[173]Helena Deutsch, *The Psychology of Women, Volume I, Girlhood* (New York: Bantam Press, 1973), p. 12.

[174]Rothman, Chapter 5; Ryan, pp. 260–261. By the 1950s, the subject of clothing has become a serious academic one in departments of home economics. See Mary Shaw Ryan, *Clothing: A Study in Human Behavior* (New York: Holt, Rinehart and Winston, 1966); and James R. McGovern, The American woman's pre-

World War I freedom in manners and morals, *The Journal of American History* 55 (September, 1968): 315–333.

[175]Christopher Lasch, *The Culture of Narcissism: America in Age of Diminishing Expectations* (New York: Norton, 1979), pp. 180–181.

[176]Gilbert and Gubar suggest that women who "self-mutilate" themselves into conventional beauty are approved by men who fear them as reminders of life, hence of mortal being. Such a woman has "eternal lineaments fixed on her, like a mask to conceal her dreadful and bloody link to Nature," p. 13. They go on to speak of "mirror madness... [which] testifies to the efforts women have expended not just trying to be angels but trying *not* to become female monsters," p. 34.

[177] Showalter, *These Modern Women*, p. 14.

[178] Rothman, p. 187.

[179]Estelle B. Friedman, The New Woman: Changing views of women in the 1920s, *The Journal of American History* 61 (September 1947): 385.

[180]Dinnerstein, p. 176.

[181]Melanie Klein, *Our Adult World* (New York: Basic Books, 1963), pp. 85, 105.

[182]Frances G. Wickes, *The Inner World of Choice* (Englewood Cliffs, New Jersey: Prentice-Hall, 1976), pp. 214–215.

[183]Irene Claremont de Castillejo, *Knowing Woman* (New York: Harper and Row, 1974), pp. 76–78.

[184]Wickes, pp. 223–224, 225.

[185]Marie Louise Von Franz, *The Feminine in Fairy Tales* (New York: Spring Publishers, 1974), p. 104.

[186]Von Franz, pp. 61–63.

[187]Johnson, Heterosexuality, the father, and male dominance, p. 24.

[188]Especially psychologists and psychoanalysts. Both Donzelot and Michel Foucault, *The History of Sexuality, Vol. I* (New York: Pantheon, 1979) document how sexual "freedom" has entailed from the beginning the intervention of the helping professions into this formerly most private of spheres.

[189]As per Judge Ben B. Lindsey's suggestions. See The promise and peril of the New Freedom, in Samuel D. Schmalhausen and V. F. Calverton, eds. *Woman's Coming of Age* (New York: Horace Liverwright, Inc., 1931), pp. 447–470.

[190]Rothman, p. 217.

[191]According to Jesse Bernard, in *The Future of Motherhood* (New York: The Dial Press, 1974), it in fact intensified throughout the 1950s and 1960s.

[192]In Atherton's *Black Oxen*, 1923, a woman who has had her youth medically restored, refuses her love, since she has nevertheless lost youthful vitality, enthusiasm, and moral strength.

[193]Ewen, p. 175.

[194]Chasseguet-Smirgel, p. 283.

[195]Peter Blos, The second individuation process of adolescence, Psychoanalytic Study of the Child 22 (1967): 177.

[196]Ewen, p. 104.

[197]As Donzelot puts it, with respect to purchase of solutions to problems, a "technology of needs was established" for the privatized family, p. 69.

[198]For a discussion of the genesis of these mechanisms, see Otto Kernberg, Factors in the psychoanalytic treatment of narcissistic personalities, Journal of the American Psychoanalytic Association 18 (1970); and Heinz Kohut, Forms and transformations of narcissism, Journal of the American Psychoanalytic Association 14 (1966), and also Lasch, The Culture of Narcissism, pp. 174–175, for an explanation of how an absent father allows early fantasies of the father to dominate the development of the superego.

[199]A fascinating contemporary debate on the prevalence of such descriptions was waged by Katherine Gerould, Feminine fiction, The Saturday Review of Literature (April 11, 1936), pp. 3–4, 15, and one of our writers, Margaret Culkin Banning, The problem of popularity, The Saturday Review of Literature (May 2, 1936), pp. 3–4, 16–17.

[200]This aspect, usually implicit, is explicit in Let's Call It Love, p. 70, where the approving hero calls birthday dinners a "practical" custom.

[201]Lorine Pruette, The married woman and the part-time job, The Annals of the American Academy of Political and Social Science 143 (May, 1929): 302–303.

[202]Berkin and Norton, p. 278: "In the popular and prescriptive literature of the 1920s and even in the 1930s, the potential contradictions of the two dominant images, career woman and professional wife and mother, went largely unnoticed. The tensions did not become apparent because, in reality, the experience of work and of marriage rarely coincided . . . women did live out the two options in their imperfect forms sequentially rather than simultaneously, if they experienced both at all." This is accurate about neither the literature nor its message, which contained throughout the period two imperatives for women, never mind if they could be lived out simultaneously or not—be married; have a career. The conflict was indeed productive of psychological tensions, even if the expression they received was somewhat indirect.

[203]Showalter, These Modern Women, quotes Suzanne LaFollette's 1926 Concerning Women to this effect, p. 13. See also Sochen, p. 99.

[204]Donzelot, p. 94. This is also substantially the view of Lasch and Foucault.

[205]Sochen, p. 165. See also Cott and Pleck, p. 478.

[206]Lois W. Banner, Women in Modern America: A Brief History (New York: Harcourt Brace Jovanovich, 1974), p. 191.

[207]William H. Chafe, The American Woman: Her Changing Social, Economic, and Political Roles, 1920–1970 (New York: Oxford Univ. Press, 1978), pp. 188–189. See also Friedman, p. 343; Cott and Pleck, p. 488.

[208]Ryan, pp. 316 ff. The number of adult females in the work force went from 25% to 36%. In 1944, 75% of them were married and most were mothers of school age children. See also Degler, pp. 418–419.

[209]Banner, p. 211. See also Degler, pp. 432–433.

[210]Sochen, p. 172.

[211]Melanie Klein, *Our Adult World*, p. 105. The depressive "position" is not precisely a stage, but describes the ability of a child (or adult) to enter into *whole*–object relationships. This ability entails guilt and depression because of its very ambivalence: We have discovered we can hurt those we love. See also Kernberg, Early ego integration, pp. 240–241.

[212]Suzanne Ellery Greene, *Books for Pleasure: Popular Fiction 1914–1945* (Bowling Green, Ohio: Bowling Green Univ. Popular Press, 1974), p. 87.

Chapter Five

[213]Rothman, p. 224. The 1950s "baby boom," on which see Degler, p. 429, is another demographic fact as worthy of note, here, as the drop in American family size in the latter half of the 19th century.

[214]Jane Flax, Do feminists need Marxism? *Quest* 3 (Summer 1976): 51.

[215]Degler, p. 418. Between 1940 and 1960 the proportion of married women in the workforce almost doubled. In 1940 less than 10% of women with children under 6 held jobs; in 1975, it was 36.6%. On the other hand, in the 1950s and 1960s the largest age group entering the workforce was women over 45—who had already reared their children, p. 432.

[216]Degler, pp. 430–431.

[217]Betty Friedan, *The Feminine Mystique* (New York: Dell, 1963), Chs. 5 and 6.

[218]Both are substantially revivals of earlier forms. Hill and Loring, for example, are publishing in the former category. See Kate Ellis's review of the "new" historical romance genre, in *In These Times*, Vol. 3, No. 12 (1979).

[219]There is another related similarity to be found between this group of texts and those discussed Chapter Two: Once again British and American productions are virtually indistinguishable.

[220]Joanna Russ, Somebody's trying to kill me and I think it's my husband: The modern gothic, *Journal of Popular Culture* (Spring 1973), p. 681.

[221]This is also usually the case in the "new" historical romance.

[222]Marie-Louise Von Franz, The process of individuation, p. 191. See also Emma Jung, On the nature of animus, (1931) in Jean Strouse, ed. *Women and Analysis: Dialogues on Psychoanalytic Views of Femininity* (New York: Dell, 1974).

[223]Phyllis Greenacre, Early physical determinants in the development of the sense of identity, *Journal of the American Psychoanalytic Association* 6 (1958), p. 616. Greenacre also discusses the twin and pseudotwin fantasies associated with narcissism, including the related phenomenon of a confusion of sexual identity. These themes are illustrated in Section V of this chapter.

[224]Judith S. Kestenberg, Outside and inside, male and female, *Journal of the American Psychoanalytic Association* 16 (1968): 468.

[225]Harriet Lerner, Parental mislabeling of female genitals as a determinant of penis envy and learning inhibitions in women, *Journal of the American Psychoanalytic Association* 25 (1976): 269–283.

[226]Klein and Riviere, p. 33.

[227]Regan, p. 774, comments that the heroines of novels of romantic suspense have never lived in one house all their lives.

[228]I am indebted to Donald B. Rinsley for this description.

[229]Chasseguet-Smirgel, p. 281.

[230]Myron A. Hofer, The principles of autonomic function in the life of man and animals, Handbook of Psychiatry, 2nd ed., Vol. 4, Organic Disorders and Psychosomatic Medicine, ed. Morton F. Reiser, (New York: Basic Books, 1975), p. 548. "The core of the emotional factor in asthma is a deep dependence upon the mother" comments Leon J. Saul, in Physiological effects of emotional tension, in Hunt, ed. Personality and Behavior Disorders, p. 287. Martin Stein and Raul Schiavi, Psychophysiological respiratory disorder, in The Comprehensive Textbook of Psychiatry, 2nd ed., Vol. 2., ed. Alfred M. Freedman, et al., mention that attacks "may be stimulated by fears of retaliatory withdrawal or estrangement from a parental figure," p. 1672.

[231]Joseph C. Rheingold, The Mother, Anxiety and Death: The Catastrophic Death Complex (Boston: Little, Brown, 1967), p. 87.

[232]Heinz Kohut, The Analysis of the Self (New York: International Universities Press, 1975), p. 115.

[233]Rheingold, p. 93.

[234]See Kestenberg; Melanie K. Klein, The Oedipus Complex in light of early anxieties, Contributions (London: Hogarth Press, 1948).

[235]Phyllis Whitney, Writing the gothic novel, The Writer (February 1967), describes this character type: "The mark of his heritage is likely to show; Heathcliff, Mr. Rochester, Max de Winter—all driven, bedeviled, stern, dark men.... He is generally older than your heroine... and has experienced a good deal of living," p. 12. There is something Hemingwayesque about him, as well, as there is about the heroes of such detective fiction as that by Ross or John D. MacDonald—a stifled sentimentality, a rescuer-of-children complex which is indulged in only with much self-mockery.

[236]Not the villains, fathers, or little boys, mind you.

[237]Whatever manipulations we have performed upon consciousness in the past 15 years, significant structural change in the bourgeois family is still in the future.

[238]Lasch, The Culture of Narcissism, pp. 175, 182. But see also Poster, pp. 200–201, on the persistence of bourgeois forms of enforcing parental authority. I disagree with Lasch about the role of "permissive" child-rearing in the genesis of the personality type I am describing. It seems to me that the exclusive and intensifying responsibility for child-rearing by one woman and a phalanx of experts will do it, whatever theories it is done by. See also Davis, Ch. 5.

[239]Klein, The Oedipus Complex, p. 385.

[240]Ibid., p. 374.

[241]Gilbert and Gubar's treatment of Charlotte Bronte shows that a sensitive woman writer of an earlier day could work with these themes, just as their treatment of Mary Shelley shows that the 20th century has no monopoly on the fear of the female body's sexuality and maternality. The fact remains that popular fiction does not treat these themes until rather recently.

[242]Anita M. Mendez and Harold J. Fine, A short history of the British school of object relations and ego psychology, *Bulletin of the Menninger Clinic* 40 (1976): 358.

[243]Regan, p. 776.

[244]Harriet Lerner, The taboos against anger, *Menninger Perspective* (Winter, 1977), p. 6.

[245]Mahler et al., p. 63.

Chapter Six

[246]As Douglas puts it, "Sentimentalism provides a way to protest a power to which one has already in part capitulated," p. 12.

[247]Philip Slater, *Earthwalk* (New York: Bantam, 1975), pp. 129–130.

[248]If we look forward a century, we find most of these fictional devices at work in contemporary popular fiction, for women *and* men. The reincarnation theme has developed into a new fictional genre, that of the "occult" novel, in which the heroine's body is taken over by the ghost of her grandmother or other female ancestor or double. A variation on this theme involves a move, for a young married woman, to an old house, and a subsequent haunting which either destroys her marriage or changes it significantly. Incest is a prominent feature in recent popular fiction. An example is the best-selling *Flowers in the Attic*, a tale which describes how a selfish and beautiful mother locks her children up for three years, with predictable results. Even more common are stories of father-–daughter incest. All these stories deserve separate analysis.

[249]See Barbara Easton, Feminism and the contemporary family, in Cott and Pleck, for a treatment of new forms of masculine dominance. Like many of us, she has trouble arriving at a coherent description.

[250]Douglas dates this development from the 1870s, pp. 78–79.

[251]Berkin and Norton say of American women in the 1950s and after, "only a movement that challenged their roles in the home as well as in the workplace could have tapped [their] pain and anger . . .", p. 391.

[252]This adolescent competitiveness, not to speak of the sexual competitiveness which the consumer culture encourages, effectively blocks normal narcissism, which has a positive function in identity maintenance when it elicits action and reaction, outside the limits of the depersonalized social role. This seems to me a fair description of sexual love, as *it is not depicted* in popular women's fiction. See Heinz Lichtenstein, The role of narcissism in the emergence and maintenance of a primary identity, *The International Journal of Psycho-Analysis* 45 (January 1964): 55.

[253]This loss is also felt by the heroines of the new historical romance and the Harlequin Romance.

[254]Obviously, this statement is not descriptive of all societies.

[255]Lasch, *Haven*, pp. 131–132, and *passim*, and see also Davis's idea of what he terms the "delegated release" mode of child-rearing current in America from 1940–1965.

[256]Of course, it does not do so in popular romantic fiction either, but it pretends to.

[257]Gilbert and Gubar, pp. 439–440.

[258]Degler suggests that we are returning to a preindustrial mode, because more married women are working, as women did and do in preindustrial societies, mainly to help the family out, pp. 452–453. This interesting idea does not touch the problems of love and authority. See also Sheila B. Kammerman, Work and family in industrialized societies, *Signs* 4 (Summer 1979): 648–650, for a description of contemporary family types.

[259]Degler suggests that the period of dependency is actually extending itself in American families at present, p. 460.

[260]A branch of popular fiction that is *creating* such new images is science fiction by women. See Nina Auerbach, *Communities of Women: An Idea in Fiction* (Cambridge, Massachusetts: Harvard Univ. Press, 1978) for a treatment of such creations in 19th and 20th century British and American novels by women.

INDEX